A BIBLIOGRAPHY

OF

JAMES RUSSELL LOWELL

J. R. Lowell

A BIBLIOGRAPHY OF

JAMES RUSSELL LOWELL

COMPILED BY GEORGE WILLIS COOKE

MILFORD HOUSE
BOSTON

This Milford House book is an unabridged
republication of the edition of 1906 reprinted
from the original in Boston Public Library.

Published in 1972 by MILFORD HOUSE INC.
85 Newbury Street, Boston, Massachusetts

Library of Congress Catalogue Card Number: 78-186788
Standard Book Number: 0-87821-100-4

Printed in the United States of America

TABLE OF CONTENTS

PREFACE

AN attempt has been made in this book to give a complete list of Lowell's writings, and a selected list of what is most important that has been said about him, for the use of students, librarians, collectors, and others. No one who has any idea of what such a work implies in its preparation can anticipate that it will be complete in every particular or free from errors. The compiler has tried to avoid unnecessary blunders, and to make his work a helpful guide to those who may need it. As a literary worker he has had in mind the requirements of students rather than collectors in the arrangement of his materials. At the same time, he has anticipated the demand of the bibliographer for details and accuracy.

After a chronological list of Lowell's books, and another of Lowell bibliographies, there is given an alphabetical arrangement of his single titles, including poems, essays, criticisms, speeches, etc. In this list of single titles the place and date of the first appearance of each piece is briefly noted, also the place and date of its book publication. Important changes are noted, but no attempt has been made to give every form in which any poem or essay has appeared. In this list the prose titles have been printed in roman, the poems in italic, and the book titles in small capitals.

The early poems were in 1877 separated into "Earlier" and "Miscellaneous," and these permanent divisions have been indicated by brackets. The same has been done for "Memorial Verses" and "Poems of the War," to signify their separation from previous collections or groups.

The single works have been grouped together, in order that the various editions and other bibliographical details may be fully noted. There has been added a list of the most important criticisms, guides to study, and book-sale prices. It is hoped this arrangement will prove helpful, not only to students, but also to librarians and bibliographers. To bring everything relating to each of the books together it has been thought will prove a useful arrangement.

Under the head of complete editions will be found noted the successive additions which have been made to them, and the changes which have been made in the arrangement of titles and books. The contents of the several editions are given whenever there have been additions or rearrangements.

Since many of the notices and criticisms do not relate to particular books, an alphabetical list has been given of those most worthy of attention, which repeats those presented under the individual titles. Lowell made a large number of speeches and addresses, the titles of which it has been thought best to place together, in order that their various repetitions and publications may be noted.

Lowell frequently changed the titles of his poems. Wherever this was done they have been listed under both titles. Under each the title is given in brackets as it appeared in the periodical or book mentioned, having its place on the same line.

The exact title-page of each of Lowell's books is given as it was worded in the first edition. Following the title-page date is given that of copyright and of actual publication in brackets, in those instances where the two do not agree.

In order to make this work more nearly complete, it has been thought best to include the prices at which first editions have been sold in recent years. These vary greatly, the price depending on the condition of the book, the competing demand for it, and whether it has special features which commend it to collectors. It is impossible in many instances to recover these details, therefore the prices given are suggestive only of what the first editions are likely to bring when in good condition.

BIBLIOGRAPHY

CHRONOLOGICAL LIST OF
LOWELL'S WORKS

1838 Harvardiana. Boston.
Class Poem. Cambridge.
1841 A Year's Life. Boston.
1843 The Pioneer. Boston.
1844 Poems. Cambridge.
Conversations on Some of the Old Poets. Cambridge.
1848 Poems. Second Series. Cambridge.
A Fable for Critics. New York.
The Biglow Papers. Cambridge.
The Vision of Sir Launfal. Cambridge.
1849 Poems. 2 volumes. Boston.
1855 Poems of Maria Lowell. Cambridge.
1858 Poetical Works. Boston.
1862 Mason and Slidell: A Yankee Idyll. Boston.
1864 Fireside Travels. Boston.
1865 Ode recited at the Harvard Commemoration. Cambridge.
1867 The Biglow Papers. Second Series. Boston.
1868 Under the Willows, and Other Poems. Boston.
1870 The Cathedral. Boston.
Among My Books. Boston.
1871 My Study Windows. Boston.
1876 Among My Books. Second Series. Boston.
1877 Three Memorial Poems. Boston.
Complete Poetical Works. Boston.
1886 Democracy, and Other Addresses. Boston.
1888 The Independent in Politics. New York.
Political Essays. Boston.
Heartsease and Rue. Boston.

1890 Writings of James Russell Lowell, Riverside Edition,
      10 volumes. Boston.

1891 Latest Literary Essays and Addresses. Boston.

1892 The Old English Dramatists. Boston.

1893 Letters. Edited by Charles Eliot Norton. New
      York.

1895 Last Poems. Edited by Charles Eliot Norton. Bos-
      ton.

1896 The Power of Sound: A Rhymed Lecture. New
      York.

1897 Lectures on the English Poets. Cleveland.

1899 Impressions of Spain. Boston.

1902 Anti-Slavery Papers. Boston.
      Early Prose Writings. New York.

1904 Complete Writings, Elmwood Edition, 16 volumes.
      Boston.

BIBLIOGRAPHIES OF LOWELL

ARNOLD, WILLIAM HARRIS. First Editions of Bryant, Emerson, Hawthorne, Lowell, Thoreau, Whittier. Lowell, pp. 74–90.

DURGEE, GEORGE W. W. First Editions of Lowell. Book-buyer, July, 1899, v. 18, p. 436.

FOLEY, PATRICK KEVIN. American Authors, 1795–1895: a Bibliography of First and Notable Editions, chrono-logically arranged, with Notes. 1897. Lowell, pp. 180–187.

HALE, EDWARD EVERETT, JR. Life of James Russell Lowell. Boston, Small, Maynard & Co., 1899. Biblio-graphy, pp. 124–128.

HOWE, MARK ANTONY DeWOLFE. First Editions of Whittier and Lowell. Bookman, March, 1898, v. 7, p. 35.
American Bookmen, "First Editions of Whittier and Lowell." New York, Dodd, Mead & Co., 1898.

JONES, GARDNER MAYNARD. Special Reading List of Lowell. Bulletin Salem Public Library, March, 1901, v. 5, no. 19.

LITERARY WORLD. Bibliography of Lowell, June 27, 1885, v. 16, p. 225.
List of Lowell's Books, August 29, 1891, v. 22, p. 297.
First Editions of Fable for Critics, January 8, 22, March 5, 1898, v. 29, pp. 9, 26, 74.

LIVINGSTON, LUTHER S. First Books of some American Authors. Bookman, October, 1898, v. 8, p. 138.

SCUDDER, HORACE ELISHA. James Russell Lowell: A Biography. Boston, Houghton, Mifflin & Co., 1901. List of Lowell's Writings arranged in order of pub-lication, v. 2, pp. 421–447.

SCUDDER, HORACE ELISHA.   Complete Poetical Works, Cambridge Ed. Boston, Houghton, Mifflin & Co., 1896.   A Chronological list of Mr. Lowell's Poems. In Appendix, pp. 481–484.

STONE, HERBERT STUART.   First Editions of American Authors: a Manual for Book-Lovers.   Lowell, pp. 130–132.

UNDERWOOD, FRANCIS HENRY.   James Russell Lowell. The Poet and the Man: Recollections and Appreciations.   Boston, Lee & Shepard, 1893.   Bibliography, pp. 129–133.

WHEELER, MARTHA THORNE.   Bulletin of Bibliography. Best Editions of James Russell Lowell.   Boston October, 1902, v. 3, pp. 42, 43.

ALPHABETICAL LIST OF
SINGLE TITLES

The titles of poems are given in italic, prose articles in roman, and book-titles in small capitals. If the last entry under a title is not that of one of Lowell's books now published, or a division in his Complete Poems, it indicates that that title has not been retained by the author in his authorized works. When the titles of poems or essays have been changed, both are listed, that belonging to the volume indicated being enclosed in brackets.

"A gentleness that grows of steady faith."
> A Year's Life, 1841.

Abolitionists and Emancipation, The.
> Anti-Slavery Standard, March 1, 1849.
> Anti-Slavery Papers, 1902.

Above and Below.
> The Young American, January, 1847, v. i, p. 54.
> Poems, second series, 1848.
> [Miscellaneous Poems, 1877.]

Abraham Lincoln.
> North American Review, December, 1863, v. 98, p. 241.
> [The President's Policy.]
> Political Essays, 1888.

Absence.
> Heartsease and Rue, 1888.

After the Burial.
> Atlantic Monthly, May, 1868, v. 21, p. 627.
> Letters, v. i, p. 237, on death of second child, Rose.
> Under the Willows and Other Poems, 1868.

Agassiz.
> Atlantic Monthly, May, 1874, v. 33, p. 386.
> Heartsease and Rue, 1888.

Agatha.
> Boston Miscellany, January, 1842, v. i, p. 9.

Agro-Dolce. [*To Charles Eliot Norton.*]
> Under the Willows and Other Poems, 1868.

Al Fresco.
> Anti-Slavery Standard, March 8, 1849. [A Day in June.]
> Under the Willows and Other Poems, 1868.

Aladdin.
> Under the Willows and Other Poems, 1868.

All Saints.
> Written for Harriet Ryan's Fair, March 20, 1859, 16mo,
> 1 p. Cambridge, 1859.
> Under the Willows and Other Poems, 1868.

"All things are sad."
> A Year's Life, 1841.

Allegra.
> Poems, 1844.
> [Earlier Poems, 1877.]

Ambrose.
> Anti-Slavery Standard, December 7, 1848.
> Poems, v. 2, 1849.
> [Miscellaneous Poems, 1877.]

American Dictionary of the English Language. [Webster.]
> Atlantic Monthly, May, 1860, v. 5, p. 631.

American Tract Society, The.
> Atlantic Monthly, July, 1858, v. 2, p. 246.
> Political Essays, 1888.

AMONG MY BOOKS, Boston, 1870, 1876.

Ancient Danish Ballads. [Prior.]
> Atlantic Monthly, January, 1861, v. 7, p. 124.

Anecdote of Walter Savage Landor, An.
> Sheets of the Cradle, Fair for Infant Asylum, Boston, De-
> cember 6–11, 1875. Edited by Susan Hale.

Anne. [Sonnets on Names. v.]
> A Year's Life, 1841.

Another Letter from B. Sawin, Esq.
>   Anti-Slavery Standard, September 28, 1848.
>   Biglow Papers, first series, IX.

Another Word on Mr. Webster's Speech.
>   Anti-Slavery Standard, April 4, 1850.
>   Anti-Slavery Papers, 1902.

Anti-Apis.
>   Anti-Slavery Standard, January 30, 1851.
>   Poetical Works, 1877.

Anti-Slavery Criticism upon Mr. Clay's Letter.
>   Anti-Slavery Standard, April 26, 1849.
>   Anti-Slavery Papers, 1902.

Anti-Slavery in the United States.
>   London Daily Times, February 2, March 18, April 17, May
>   18, 1846.

*Anti-Texas. Written on occasion of the Convention in
Faneuil Hall, January 29, 1845.*
>   Boston Courier, January 30, 1845. [Another Rallying Cry
>   by a Yankee.]
>   Poems, second series, 1848.

Appledore.
>   Graham's Magazine, February, 1851, v. 38, p. 87.
>   Reprinted as "Pictures from Appledore."

April Birth-day, An — at Sea.
>   Last Poems, 1895.

Arcadia Rediviva.
>   Heartsease and Rue, 1888.

Are ye truly Free? [Stanzas on Freedom.]
>   Anti-Slavery Harp; a Collection of Songs for Anti-Slavery
>   Meetings, Boston, 1849.

Astronomer Misplaced, The. [Campaign Epigrams.]
>   The Nation, October 12, 1876, v. 23, p. 224.

At Sea.
>   Leaves from my Journal, I; Fireside Travels.

At the Burns Centennial, January, 1859.
>Heartsease and Rue, 1888.

At the Commencement Dinner, 1866.
>Boston Evening Transcript, July 20, 1866.
>Heartsease and Rue, 1888.

Auf Wiedersehen! [Summer.]
>Putnam's Monthly, December, 1854, v. 4, p. 570.
>Under the Willows and Other Poems, 1868.

August Afternoon.
>The Crayon, January 3, 1855.
>Afterwards, with changes, "Pictures from Appledore," I–IV.

Auspex.
>A Masque of Poets, Boston, 1878. [My heart, I cannot still it.]
>Heartsease and Rue, 1888.

Ballad. "Gloomily the river floweth."
>Graham's Magazine, October, 1841, v. 19, p. 171.

Ballad of the Stranger, The.
>The Token and Atlantic Souvenir, Boston, 1842.

Bankside. [Home of Edmund Quincy.] Dedham, May 21, 1877.
>The Nation, May 31, 1877, v. 24, p. 318.
>Wensley and Other Stories, by Edmund Quincy, Boston, 1885.
>Heartsease and Rue, 1888.

Bartlett's " Familiar Quotations."
>North American Review, July, 1869, v. 109, p. 293.

Beatrice.
>Atlantic Monthly, June, 1858, v. 2, p. 58.
>Heartsease and Rue, 1888.   [Das Ewig-Weibliche.]

Beatrice Cenci. [Guerrazzi.]
>Atlantic Monthly, March, 1858, v. 1, p. 638.

Beaumont and Fletcher.
>Harper's Monthly, October, 1892, v. 85, p. 757.
>The Old English Dramatists, 1892.

Beaver Brook.
>   Anti-Slavery Standard, January 4, 1848. [The Mill.]
>   Poems, v. 2, 1849.

Beecher's Autobiography. [Dr. Lyman.]
>   North American Review, April, 1864, v. 98, p. 622.

Beggar, The.
>   A Year's Life, 1841.
>   Poems, v. 1, 1849.
>   [Earlier Poems, 1877.]

Bellerophon.
>   A Year's Life, 1841.

"Beloved, in the noisy city here."
>   Poems, 1844.
>   [Earlier Poems, 1877.]

Béranger. [Translation of Sainte-Beuve.]
>   Atlantic Monthly, February, 1858, v. 1, p. 469.

Bibliographical Guide to American Literature. [Trübner.]
>   Atlantic Monthly, June, 1859, v. 3, p. 775.

Bibliolatres.
>   Anti-Slavery Standard, May 24, 1849.
>   Poems, v. 2, 1849.
>   [Miscellaneous Poems, 1877.]

Biglow Papers, 1848, 1867.

Birch-Tree, The.
>   Poems, second series, 1848.

Birdofredum Sawin, Esq., to Mr. Hosea Biglow.
>   Atlantic Monthly, January, March, 1862, v. 9, pp. 126, 385.
>   Biglow Papers, second series, I.

Birthday Verses.
>   Atlantic Monthly, January, 1877, v. 39, p. 60.
>   Heartsease and Rue, 1888.

Bittersweet. [Holland.]
>   Atlantic Monthly, May, 1859, v. 3, p. 651.

Callirhöe.
>Graham's Magazine, March, 1841, p. 100.

Cambridge Thirty Years Ago. [A Memoir addressed to Edelmann Storg (W. W. Story) in Rome.]
>Putnam's Monthly, April, May, 1853, v. 3, pp. 379, 473.
>Fireside Travels, 1864.

Campaign Epigrams.
>The Nation, September 14, October 12, 1876, v. 23, pp. 163, 224.
>Partly in Heartsease and Rue, 1888.

Canada.
>Anti-Slavery Standard, November 1, 1849.
>Anti-Slavery Papers, 1902.

Captive, The.
>The Missionary Memorial: A Literary and Religious Souvenir, New York, 1846.
>Poems, second series, 1848.
>[Miscellaneous Poems, 1877.]

Carlyle. 1866.
>North American Review, April, 1866, v. 152, p. 419.
>My Study Windows, 1871.

Caroline. [Sonnets on Names. IV.]
>A Year's Life, 1841.

Casa sin Alma. Recuerdo de Madrid.
>Heartsease and Rue, 1888.

CATHEDRAL, THE.
>Atlantic Monthly, January, 1870, v. 25, p. 1.
>Boston, Fields, Osgood & Co., 1870.
>Poetical Works, 1877.

Changed Perspective.
>Heartsease and Rue, 1888.

Changeling, The.
>Poems, v. 2, 1849.
>[Miscellaneous Poems, 1877.]

Chapman.
>   Harper's Magazine, September, 1892, v. 85, p. 561.
>   The Old English Dramatists, 1892.

Chaucer.
>   North American Review, July, 1870, v. 111, p. 155.
>   My Study Windows, 1871.

Chippewa Legend, A.
>   The Liberty Bell, 1844.
>   Poems, 1844.
>   [Miscellaneous Poems, 1877.]

Christmas Carol, A. [For the Sunday-school Children of the Church of the Disciples.]
>   Heartsease and Rue, 1888.

Church, The.
>   A Year's Life, 1841.

Church and Clergy, The.
>   Pennsylvania Freeman, February 27, 1845.
>   Anti-Slavery Papers, 1902.

Church and Clergy Again.
>   Pennsylvania Freeman, March 27, 1845.
>   Anti-Slavery Papers, 1902.

Church's "Legende of Goode Women."
>   North American Review, April, 1864, v. 98, p. 626.

Class Day.
>   Harvard Book, Boston, 1878.

CLASS POEM.
>   Cambridge, 1838.

Coincidence, A. [Campaign Epigrams.]
>   The Nation, September 14, v. 23, p. 163.

Coleridge.
>   Address on unveiling bust at Westminster Abbey, May 1885.
>   Literary and Political Addresses, 1890.

Collins's "Voyage Down the Amoor."
>   Atlantic Monthly, June, 1860, v. 5, p. 757.

Columbus.

> Poems, second series, 1848.
> [Miscellaneous Poems, 1877.]

Compromise.

> Anti-Slavery Standard, March 1, 1850.
> Anti-Slavery Papers, 1902.

Conduct of Life. [Emerson.]

> Atlantic Monthly, February, 1861, v. 7, p. 254.

" Conquerors of the New World and their Bondsmen, The."

> Anti-Slavery Standard, October 12, 26, 1848.
> Anti-Slavery Papers, 1902.

Contrast, A.

> Liberty Chimes, Providence, 1845.
> Poems, second series, 1848.
> [Miscellaneous Poems, 1877.]

CONVERSATIONS ON SOME OF THE OLD POETS.

> Cambridge, 1844.

Copeland's "Country Life."

> Atlantic Monthly, p. 384, September, 1859, v. 4, p. 254.

Course of the Whigs, The.

> Anti-Slavery Standard, January 11, 1849.
> Anti-Slavery Papers, 1902.

Courtin', The.

> Biglow Papers, first series, 1848. Notices of an Independent Press.

Courtship of Miles Standish, The. [Longfellow.]

> Atlantic Monthly, February, 1859, v. 3, p. 129.

Credidimus Jovem Regnare.

> Atlantic Monthly, February, 1887, v. 59, p. 246.
> Heartsease and Rue, 1888.

Criticism and Abuse.

> Anti-Slavery Standard, September 20, 1849.
> Anti-Slavery Papers, 1902.

Criticism and Culture.

> Century, February, 1894, v. 25 n. s., p. 515.

Curven's Journal and Letters.
North American Review, January, 1865, v. 100 p. 288.

Dancing Bear, The.
Atlantic Monthly, September, 1875, v. 36, p. 329.
Heartsease and Rue, 1888.

Daniel Webster.
Anti-Slavery Standard, July 2, 1846.
Anti-Slavery Papers, 1902.

Dante.
Appleton's New American Encyclopedia, 1870.
Fifth Annual Report, Dante Society, 1886.
Among My Books, second series, 1876.

Dara.
Graham's Magazine, July, 1850, v. 37, p. 7.
Under the Willows, 1868.

Darkened Mind, The.
Under the Willows and Other Poems, 1868.

Das Ewig-Weibliche.
Atlantic Monthly, June, 1858, v. 2, p. 58. [Beatrice.]
Heartsease and Rue, 1888.

David Gray's Poems, with Memoir of his Life.
North American Review, October, 1864, v. 99. p. 627.

Day in June, A.
Anti-Slavery Standard, March 8, 1849.
Under the Willows and Other Poems, 1868. [Al Fresco.]

Day of Small Things, The.
Anti-Slavery Standard, October 16, 1848.
Memorial Verses, Poetical Works, 1857. [To W. L. Garrison.]

Dead House, The.
Atlantic Monthly, October, 1858, v. 2, p. 618.
Under the Willows and Other Poems, 1868.

Dead Letter, A.
Harvardiana, May, 1838, p. 317.

Death of Queen Mercedes.
Heartsease and Rue, 1888.

Debate in the Sennit, The.
  Boston Courier, May 3, 1848.
  Biglow Papers, first series, v.

Defrauding Nature. [Campaign Epigrams.]
  The Nation, September 14, 1876, v. 23, p. 163.

DEMOCRACY.
  Inaugural Address Midland Institute, October 6, 1884.
  Democracy and Other Addresses, 1886.

Departed, The.
  A Year's Life, 1841.

[Dickens's "American Notes."]
  The Pioneer, January, 1843.

Dictionary of Americanisms.
  Atlantic Monthly, November, 1859, v. 4, p. 638.

Dictionary of Authors. [Allibcne.]
  Atlantic Monthly, June, 1859, v. 3, p. 775.

Dictionary of English Etymology. [Wedgwood.]
  Atlantic Monthly, August, 1860, v. 6, p. 248.

Dictionary of the English Language. [Worcester.]
  Atlantic Monthly, May, 1860, v. 5, p. 631.

Dies Irae. [Coles.]
  Atlantic Monthly, June, 1860, v. 5, p. 752.

Diplomatic Correspondence.
  North American Review, April, 1864, v. 98, p. 619.

Diplomatic Letters from Spain.
  Critic, "Mr. Lowell in Spain," September, 1898, v. 33, p. 171.
  Century, "Lowell's Impressions of Spain," November, 1898, v. 57, p. 140.
  Impressions of Spain, New York, 1899.

Dirge, A.
  Graham's Magazine, July, 1842, v. 21, p. 31.
  Poems, 1844.

Discovery, The.
  Heartsease and Rue, 1888.

Disquisition on Foreheads. By Job Simifrans.
>   Boston Miscellany, March, 1842, v. 1, p. 134.
>   Early Prose Writings, 1902.

Disraeli's "Tancred, or the New Crusade."
>   North American Review, July, 1847, v. 65, p. 201.

Don Quixote.
>   At Workingmen's College, London.
>   Democracy and Other Addresses, 1886.

Dramatic Works of John Webster.
>   Atlantic Monthly, June, 1858, v. 2, p. 119.

Dream I Had, A.
>   National Anti-Slavery Standard, November 28, 1850.

Dryden.
>   North American Review, July, 1868, v. 107, p. 186.
>   Among My Books, first series, 1870.

E. G. de R.
>   Heartsease and Rue, 1888.

E Pluribus Unum.
>   Atlantic Monthly, February, 1861, v. 7, p. 235.
>   Political Essays, 1888.

EARLIER POEMS.
>   Division made in Complete Poems, 1877.

Edgar Allan Poe. "Our Contributors." No. xvii. "Edgar Allan Poe."
>   Graham's Magazine, February, 1845, v. 27, p. 49.
>   Griswold's ed. of Poe.
>   Stoddard's Works of Poe, v. 1, p. 201.
>   Woodberry's ed. of Poe, v. 10, p. 247.

Edinburgh Papers. [Chambers.]
>   Atlantic Monthly, January, 1861, v. 7, p. 125.

Edith. [Sonnets on Names. I.]
>   A Year's Life, 1841.

El Dorado.
>   Anti-Slavery Papers, December 14, 1848.

Eleanor makes Macaroons.
    Heartsease and Rue, 1888.

Election in November, The.
    Atlantic Monthly, October, 1860, v. 6, p. 492.
    Political Essays, 1888.

Elegy on the Death of Dr. Channing.
    The Liberty Bell, 1843.
    Poems, 1844.
    [Memorial Verses, 1857.]

Elsie Venner. [Holmes.]
    Atlantic Monthly, April, 1861, v. 7, p. 509.

Ember Picture, An.
    Atlantic Monthly, July, 1867, v. 20, p. 99.
    Under the Willows and Other Poems, 1868.

Emerson the Lecturer.
    The Nation, November 12, 1868, v. 7, p. 389.
    My Study Windows, 1871.

Endymion; a Mystical Comment on Titian's "Sacred and Profane Love."
    Atlantic Monthly, February, 1888, v. 61, p. 261.

Epigram on Certain Conservatives, An.
    Broadway Journal, January 25, 1845.

Epigram on J. M.
    Atlantic Monthly, May, 1858, v. 1, p. 846.

Epistle to George William Curtis, An.
    Heartsease and Rue, 1888.

Epitaph, An.
    The Nation, October 1, 1874, v. 19, p. 216.

Epitaph, The. "What means this glosing epitaph?"
    Broadway Journal, January 11, 1845, p. 28.
    Poems, second series, 1848.

Estrangement.
    Century, May, 1882, v. 2 n. s., p. 16.
    Heartsease and Rue, 1888.

Eternal One, The.
> Arcturus, May, 1842, p. 407.

Ethnology.
> Anti-Slavery Standard, February 1, 1849.
> Anti-Slavery Papers, 1902.

Eurydice.
> Anti-Slavery Standard, August 23, 1849.
> Poems, v. 2, 1849.
> [Miscellaneous Poems, 1877.]

Exciting Intelligence from South Carolina.
> Anti-Slavery Standard, September 7, 1848.
> Anti-Slavery Papers, 1902.

Ex-Mayor's Crumb of Consolation, The; a Pathetic Ballad.
> Anti-Slavery Standard, October 26, 1848.

Extract, An.
> The Liberty Bell, 1848.

Extreme Unction.
> The Liberty Bell, 1847.
> Poems, second series, 1848.
> [Miscellaneous Poems, 1877.]

Eye's Treasury, The.
> Heartsease and Rue, 1888.

FABLE FOR CRITICS, A.
> New York, 1848.

Fact or Fancy?
> Atlantic Monthly, March, 1887, v. 59, p. 289.
> Heartsease and Rue, 1888.

Falcon, The.
> The Liberty Bell, 1847. [The Falconer.]
> Poems, second series, 1848.
> Poems, v. 1, 1849. [The Falcon.]
> [Miscellaneous Poems, 1877.]

Familiar Epistle to a Friend, A. [Miss Jane Norton.]
> Atlantic Monthly, April, 1867, v. 19, p. 488.
> Under the Willows and Other Poems, 1868.

Fanaticism in the Navy.
>Anti-Slavery Standard, August 31, 1848.
>Anti-Slavery Papers, 1902.

Fancies about a Rosebud. Pressed in an Old Copy of Spenser.
>Graham's Magazine, March, 1842, v. 20, p. 173.
>Poems, v. 1, 1849.

Fancy's Casuistry.
>Under the Willows and Other Poems, 1868.

Fantasy, A.
>Boston Miscellany, July, 1842, v. 2, p. 15.
>Poems, 1844.

Fatal Curiosity, The.
>Victoria Regia, edited by Adelaide A. Proctor, London, 1861, Emily Faithfull & Co.

Fatherland, The.
>Democratic Review, October, 1843, v. 13, p. 430.
>Poems, v. 1, 1849.
>[Earlier Poems, 1877.]

Farewell.
>Graham's Magazine, June, 1842, v. 20, p. 305.

Feeling, A.
>A Year's Life, 1841.

Festina Lente.
>Atlantic Monthly, April, 1862, v. 9, p. 512.
>Biglow Papers, second series, IV.

Few Bits of Roman Mosaic, A.
>Leaves from my Journal, IV. Fireside Travels.

Fielding.
>Address at Taunton, September 4, 1883.
>Democracy and Other Addresses, 1886.

Fiery Trial, The.
>The Liberty Bell, 1842.
>Poems, 1844.

Finding of the Lyre, The.
> Under the Willows and Other Poems, 1868.

FIRESIDE TRAVELS.
> Boston, 1864.

First Client, The; with Incidental Good Precepts for Incipient Attorneys.
> Boston Miscellany, May, 1842, p. 228.
> Early Prose Writings, 1902.

First Lesson in Natural History, A.
> Atlantic Monthly, December, 1859, v. 4, p. 773.

First Snow-Fall, The.
> Anti-Slavery Standard, December 27, 1849.
> Memory and Hope, Boston, 1850.
> The Crayon, January 31, 1855, v. 1, p. 73.   (Revised by author.)
> Under the Willows and Other Poems, 1868.

Fitz Adam's Story.
> Atlantic Monthly, January, 1867, v. 19, p. 17.
> Part of "The Nooning," written about 1850.
> Heartsease and Rue, 1888.

Five Indispensable Authors, The.
> Century, December, 1893, v. 25 n. s., p. 223.

Flowers.
> Southern Literary Messenger, July, 1840, v. 6, p. 579.
> A Year's Life, 1841.

Flying Dutchman, The.
> Atlantic Monthly, January, 1869, v. 23, p. 27.
> Heartsease and Rue, 1888.

Follower, The.
> The Pioneer, January, 1843, p. 41.

Footpath, The.
> Atlantic Monthly, August, 1868, v. 22, p. 252.
> Under the Willows and Other Poems, 1868.

For an Autograph.
> Under the Willows and Other Poems, 1868.

Foreboding, A.
Heartsease and Rue, 1888.

Forest Hymn, A. [Bryant.]
Atlantic Monthly, December, 1860, v. 6, p. 761.

Forgetfulness.
Anti-Slavery Standard, September 7, 1843.
Poems, 1844.

Forlorn, The.
Poems, 1844.
[Earlier Poems, 1877.]

Forster's "Swift."
The Nation, April 13, 20, 1876, v. 22, pp. 248, 265.

Forty-four Years of the Life of a Hunter, being Reminiscences of Meshach Browning.
Atlantic Monthly, December, 1859, v. 4, p. 770.

Fountain, The.
Poems, v. 1, 1849.
[Earlier Poems, 1877.]

Fountain of Youth, The.
Putnam's Monthly, January, 1853, v. 1, p. 45.
Under the Willows and Other Poems, 1868.

Fourth of July in Charleston.
Anti-Slavery Standard, July 26, 1849.
Anti-Slavery Papers, 1902.

Fourth of July Ode.
Anti-Slavery Standard, July 1, 1841.
A Year's Life, 1841.

Fragments.
Century, May, 1894, v. 26 n. s., p. 24.

Fragments of an Unfinished Poem.
Putnam's Monthly, April, 1853, v. 1, p. 403.
Part of "Our Own: His Wanderings and Personal Adventures."
Riverside Ed., v. 3, 1890.

" Franciscus de Verulamio sic cogitavit."
Heartsease and Rue, 1888.

Francis Parkman.
Century, November, 1892, v. 23 n. s., p. 44.

Freedom.
Anti-Slavery Standard, June 15, 1848.
Poems, v. 2, 1849.
[Miscellaneous Poems, 1877.]

French Revolution of 1848, The.
Anti-Slavery Standard, April 13, 1848.
Anti-Slavery Papers, 1902.

From a " Hasty Pudding Poem."
Harvardiana, June, 1838, p. 343.

" Full many noble friends."
Poems, 1844.

Function of the Poet, The.
Century, January, 1894, v. 25 n. s., p. 432.

Garfield.
Memorial meeting in London, September 24, 1881.
Democracy and Other Addresses, 1886.

General Bem's Conversion.
Anti-Slavery Standard, December 6, 1849.
Anti-Slavery Papers, 1902.

General McClellan's Report [on the Army of the Potomac].
North American Review, April, 1864, v. 98, p. 550.
Political Essays, 1888.

General Taylor.
Anti-Slavery Standard, March 15, 1849.
Anti-Slavery Papers, 1902.

Getting Up.
Boston Miscellany, March, 1842, v. 1, p. 111.
Early Prose Writings, 1902.

Ghost Seer, The.
  The Broadway Journal, March 8, 1845.
  Poems, v. 2, 1849.
  [Miscellaneous Poems, 1877.]

Glance behind the Curtain, A.
  Democratic Review, September, 1843, v. 13, p. 236.
  Poems, 1844.
  [Miscellaneous Poems, 1877.]

Godminster Chimes. [Written in aid of a chime of bells
  for Christ Church, Cambridge.]
  Poetry of the Bells, Cambridge, 1858.
  Under the Willows and Other Poems, 1868.

"*Goe, Little Booke.*"
  A Year's Life, 1841.

Gold Egg; a Dream Fantasy.
  Atlantic Monthly, May, 1865, v. 15, p. 528.
  Under the Willows and Other Poems, 1868.

Goodwin's Plutarch's Morals.
  North American Review, April, 1871, v. 112, p. 460.

Good Word for Winter, A.
  The Atlantic Almanac for 1870, Boston, 1869.
  My Study Windows, 1871.

Gray.
  New Princeton Review, March, 1886, v. 1, p. 153.
  Latest Literary Essays and Addresses, 1891.

"*Great human nature.*"
  A Year's Life, 1841.

Great Public Character, A. [Josiah Quincy.]
  Atlantic Monthly, November, 1867, v. 20, p. 618.
  My Study Windows, 1871.

"*Great truths are portions of the soul of man.*"
  The Liberty Bell, 1842.
  Poems, 1844.
  [Earlier Poems, 1877.]

Green Mountains.
   A Year's Life, 1841.

Growth of the Legend, The. A Fragment.
   Poems, second series, 1848.
   [Miscellaneous Poems, 1877.]

Hakon's Lay.
   Graham's Magazine, January, 1855, v. 46, p. 72.

Halleck's "Alnwick Castle."
   Broadway Journal, May 3, 1844.

Happiness.
   Atlantic Monthly, April, 1858, v. 1, p. 685.

Happy Martyrdom, The.
   The Liberty Bell, 1845.

Harvard Anniversary.
   Address in Sanders Theatre, November 8, 1886.
   Democracy and Other Addresses, 1886.

Haven, The.
   Poems, 1844.

[Hawthorne's "Historical Tales for Youth."]
   The Pioneer, January, 1843.

Hawthorne's "The Marble Faun."
   Atlantic Monthly, April, 1860, v. 5, p. 509.

Hazlitt's "Library of Old Authors."
   North American Review, April, 1870, v. 110, p. 444.

Hazlitt's "Poems of Richard Lovelace."
   North American Review, July, 1864, v. 99, p. 310.

HEARTSEASE AND RUE.
   Boston, 1888.

Hebe.
   The Young American, May, 1847, v. 1, p. 143.
   Poems, second series, 1848.
   [Miscellaneous Poems, 1877.]

Heritage, The.
> Poems, 1844.
> [Earlier Poems, 1877.]

His Ship.
> Harper's Magazine, December, 1891, v. 84, p. 141.

History and Description of New England (Coolidge and Mansfield).
> Atlantic Monthly, November, 1859, v. 4, p. 645.

Hob Gobling's Song.
> Our Young Folks, January, 1867.

Home Ballads and Poems. [Whittier.]
> Atlantic Monthly, November, 1860, v. 6, p. 637.

Homeric Translation in Theory and Practice. [Newman.]
> Atlantic Monthly, January, 1862, v. 9, p. 142.

"Hope first the gentle Poet leads."
> A Year's Life, 1841. [Preface.]

Hosea and the Recruiting Sergeant.
> American Anti-Slavery Almanac for 1847, New York, 1846.
> Biglow Papers, first series, i.

Howe's "Trip to Cuba."
> Atlantic Monthly, April, 1860, v. 5, p. 510.

Howells's "Venetian Life."
> North American Review, October, 1866, v. 103, p. 611.

How I Consulted the Oracle of the Goldfishes.
> Atlantic Monthly, August, 1889, v. 64, p. 145.
> Last Poems, 1895.

"How oft do I live o'er."
> Poems, 1844.

Humor, Wit, Fun and Satire.
> Century, November, 1893, v. 25 n. s., p. 125.

Hunger and Cold.
> Poems, second series, 1848.
> [Miscellaneous Poems, 1877.]

Hymn.

> Proceedings of the Anti-Slavery Meeting held in Stacy Hall,
> Boston, on the Twentieth Anniversary of the Mob of Octo-
> ber 21, 1835. Boston, published by R. F. Walcutt, 1855.

Ianthe.

> Southern Literary Messenger, July, 1840, v. 6, p. 545.
> A Year's Life, 1841.

"*I ask not for those thoughts.*"

> Poems, 1844.
> [Earlier Poems, 1877.]

"*I cannot think that thou shouldst pass away.*"

> Poems, 1844.
> [Earlier Poems, 1877.]

"*I fain would give to thee.*"

> A Year's Life, 1841.

"*If some small savor creep into my rhymes.*"

> Graham's Magazine, February, 1842, v. 20, p. 90.

"*If ye have not the one great lesson learned.*"

> The Liberty Bell, 1842.

"*I grieve not that ripe knowledge.*"

> Poems, 1844.
> [Earlier Poems, 1877.]

"*I love those poets of whatever creed.*"

> Arcturus, May, 1842, p. 407.

Il Pesceballo. [By F. J. Child.]

> Translation by Lowell, Cambridge, 1862.

Imaginary Conversation, An.

> Anti-Slavery Standard, May 18, 1848.
> Anti-Slavery Papers, 1902.

Imagination, The.

> Century, March, 1894, v. 25 n. s., p. 716.

Impartiality.

> A Year's Life, 1841.

Impatience and Reproof.
> Poems, 1844.

IMPRESSIONS OF SPAIN.
> Diplomatic correspondence, 1878. House of Representatives, 45th Congress, 3d Session, Executive Documents, v. i.
> Century, "Lowell's Impressions of Spain," November, 1898, v. 57, p. 140.
> Critic, "Mr. Lowell in Spain," September, 1898, v. 33, p. 171.
> Impressions of Spain, edited by Joseph B. Gilder, Boston, 1899.

In Absence.
> Poems, 1844.
> [Earlier Poems, 1877.]

In a Copy of "Among My Books."
> Atlantic Monthly, December, 1890, v. 86, p. 721.

In a Copy of "Fireside Travels."
> Atlantic Monthly, December, 1890, v. 86, p. 721.

In a Copy of Omar Khayyám.
> Heartsease and Rue, 1888.

In a Copy of Shakespeare.
> Century, November, 1899, v. 59, p. 49.

In a Gift Copy of Lowell's Poems.
> Atlantic Monthly, December, 1890, v. 86, p. 721.

In an Album.
> Heartsease and Rue, 1888.

In a Volume of Sir Thomas Browne.
> Atlantic Monthly, July, 1890, v. 86, p. 63.

Incident in a Railroad Car, An.
> Democratic Review, October, 1842, v. 11, p. 431.
> Poems, 1844.
> Poetry of the Bells, Cambridge, 1858.
> [Miscellaneous Poems, 1877.]

Incident of the Fire at Hamburg, An.
> Graham's Magazine, May, 1845, v. 27, p. 205.
> Poems, second series, 1848.
> [Miscellaneous Poems, 1877.]

Introduction to Whittier's "Texas: Voice of New England."
> Boston Courier, April 17, 1844.

Invita Minerva.
> The Crayon, May 30, 1855, v. 1, p. 346.
> Under the Willows and Other Poems, 1868.

Invitation to J[ohn] F[rancis] H[eath], An.
> Graham's Magazine, December, 1850, v. 37, p. 360.
> Under the Willows and Other Poems, 1868.

Irené.
> A Year's Life, 1841.
> [Earlier Poems, 1877.]

Irish and American Patriots.
> Anti-Slavery Standard, November 30, 1848.
> Anti-Slavery Papers, 1902.

Irish Rebellion, The.
> Anti-Slavery Standard, August 24, 1848.
> Anti-Slavery Papers, 1902.

Isabel.
> Southern Literary Messenger, June, 1840, v. 6, p. 468.
> A Year's Life, 1841.

"I saw a gate."
> A Year's Life, 1841.

Italy.
> Leaves from my Journal, iii. Fireside Travels.

Italy, 1859.
> Atlantic Monthly, December, 1859, v. 4, p. 738.
> Under the Willows and Other Poems, 1868. [Villa Franca.]

James's "Sketches."
> The Nation, June 17, 1875, v. 20, p. 425.

Jeffries Wyman. Died September 4, 1874.
> The Nation, October 8, 1874, v. 19, p. 234.
> Heartsease and Rue, 1888.

Jonathan to John.
>Biglow Papers, second series, II.

Joseph Winlock. Died June 11, 1875.
>The Nation, June 17, 1875, v. 20, p. 405.
>Heartsease and Rue, 1888.

Judd's " Philo."
>Anti-Slavery Standard, January 24, 1850.

July reviewed by September [with W. B. Rogers].
>Atlantic Monthly, September, 1860, v. 6, p. 378.

June Idyll, A.
>Atlantic Monthly, June, 1868, v. 21, p. 754.
>Under the Willows and Other Poems, 1868.   [Under the Willows.]

Keats.
>Introduction to Keats's Poems, Little, Brown & Co., Boston, 1854.
>Among My Books, second series, 1876.

Kettelopotomachia.
>Biglow Papers, second series, VIII.

King Retro.
>Anti-Slavery Standard, May 10, 1849.

Landlord, The.
>The People's Journal, September 4, 1847, v. 4, p. 135.
>Poems, v. 2, 1848.
>[Miscellaneous Poems, 1877.]

LAST POEMS.
>Boston, 1895.

Late Mrs. Ann Benson Proctor, The.
>The Nation, March 29, 1888, v. 46, p. 255.

LATEST LITERARY ESSAYS AND ADDRESSES.
>Boston, 1891.

Latest Views of Mr. Biglow.
>Atlantic Monthly, February, 1863, v. 11, p. 260.
>Biglow Papers, second series, VII.

Leaves from my Journal in Italy and Elsewhere.
Graham's Monthly, April, May, June, 1854.
Fireside Travels, 1864.

Leaving the Matter Open, a Tale of Homer Wilbur, A.M.
Anti-Slavery Standard, July 27, 1848.
Biglow Papers, first series, Introduction.

Lectures on the Science of Language. [Müller.]
Atlantic Monthly, January, 1862, v. 9, p. 140.

Legend of Brittany, A.
Poems, 1844.
[Miscellaneous Poems, 1877.]

L'Envoi.
Poems, 1844.
[Earlier Poems, 1877.]

L'Envoi. To the Muse.
Atlantic Monthly, March, 1860, v. 5, p. 310.
Under the Willows and Other Poems, 1868.

Leslie's Autobiographical Recollections.
Atlantic Monthly, September, 1860, v. 6, p. 373.

Lessing.
North American Review, April, 1867, v. 104, p. 541.
Among My Books, first series, 1870.

Lesson, The.
Heartsease and Rue, 1888.

Lesson of the Pine, The.
Anti-Slavery Standard, November 15, 1849.
Under the Willows and Other Poems, 1868. [A Mood.]

Letter from a Candidate for the Presidency, A.
Anti-Slavery Standard, June 1, 1848.
Biglow Papers, first series, vii.

Letter from a Volunteer in Saltillo.
Boston Courier, August 18, 1847.
Biglow Papers, first series, ii.

Letter from Boston. December, 1846.
> Anti-Slavery Standard, January 2, 1848.
> Atlantic Monthly, April, 1884, v. 53, p. 576.
> Riverside Ed., v. 1, 1890.

*Letter from Mr. Ezekiel Biglow of Jaalam to the Hon.
Joseph T. Buckingham, A.*
> Boston Courier, June 17, 1846.
> Biglow Papers, first series, I.

Letter to my dear Sarah, A very Pleasant.
> Printed on Cardboard, n. d.

LETTERS.
> New York, 1894.
> Two volumes.

Library of Old Authors.
> Atlantic Monthly, April, May, 1858, v. 1, pp. 760, 883.
> My Study Windows, 1871.

Life and Letters of Percival.
> North American Review, January, 1867, v. 104, p. 278.
> My Study Windows, 1871.

Life of Andrew Jackson. [Parton.]
> Atlantic Monthly, March, 1861, v. 7, p. 381.

"*Light of mine eyes.*"
> A Year's Life, 1841.

"*Like some black mountain glooming huge aloof.*"
> Boston Miscellany, February, 1842, v. 1, p. 54.

Lines on the Death of Charles Turner Torrey.
> Boston Courier, May 23, 1846.
> Poems, second series, 1848.
> [Memorial Poems, 1877.]

*Lines suggested by the Graves of Two English Soldiers on
Concord Battle-Ground.*
> Anti-Slavery Standard, March 29, 1849.
> Poems, v. 2, 1849.
> [Miscellaneous Poems, 1877.]

Longfellow's "Courtship of Miles Standish."
> Atlantic Monthly, January, 1859, v. 3, p. 129.

Longfellow's "Kavanagh:" Nationality in Literature.
North American Review, July, 1849.

Longfellow's "Poems on Slavery."
The Pioneer, February, 1843.

Longfellow's "Tales of a Wayside Inn."
North American Review, January, 1864, v. 98, p. 289.

Longing.
Poems, second series, 1848.
[Miscellaneous Poems, 1877.]

Look Before and After, A.
North American Review, January, 1869, v. 108, p. 255.
[Lowell's from p. 260.]

Lord Derby's Translation of the Iliad.
North American Review, July, 1865, v. 101, p. 303.

Lost Child, The.
A Year's Life, 1841.

Love. "True love is but a humble, low-born thing."
Poems, 1844.
[Earlier Poems, 1877.]

Love and Thought.
Last Poems, 1895.

Loved One, The.
Anti-Slavery Standard, December 16, 1841.

Love-Dream, A.
A Year's Life, 1841.

Lover, The.
A Year's Life, 1841.

Love's Altar.
A Year's Life, 1841.

Loves and Heroines of the Poets.
Atlantic Monthly, December, 1860, v. 6, p. 761.

Love's Clock. A Pastoral.
Heartsease and Rue, 1888.

Love-Song.
> A Year's Life, 1841.

Lowell's "Fresh Hearts that failed Three Thousand Years ago."
> Atlantic Monthly, June, 1860, v. 5, p. 759.

Lowell's Letters to Poe.
> Scribner's Magazine, August, 1894, v. 16, p. 170.

Lyrics of a Day.
> North American Review, July, 1864, v. 99, p. 320.

Macaulay's "Lays of Ancient Rome."
> The Pioneer, February, 1843.

Mahmood the Image-Breaker.
> Anti-Slavery Standard, April 18, 1850.
> Under the Willows and Other Poems, 1868.

Maple, The.
> Atlantic Monthly, November, 1857, v. 1, p. 120.
> Heartsease and Rue, 1888.

Marlowe.
> Harper's Magazine, July, 1892, v. 85, p. 194.
> The Old English Dramatists, 1892.

Married Men: by One who knows them.
> Boston Miscellany, August, 1842, v. 2, p. 116.
> Early Prose Writings, 1902.

Marsh's Lectures on the English Language.
> Atlantic Monthly, April, 1860, v. 5, p. 508.

Marsh's "Man and Nature."
> North American Review, July, 1864, v. 99, p. 319.

Mary. [Sonnets on Names.]
> A Year's Life, 1841.

Masaccio. In the Brancacci Chapel.
> Knickerbocker Gallery; a Testimonial to the Editor of the Knickerbocker Magazine from its Contributors. New York, Samuel Hueston, 1855.
> Under the Willows and Other Poems, 1868.

Mason and Slidell; a Yankee Idyll.
> Atlantic Monthly, February, 1862, v. 9, p. 259.
> Reprint, Boston, 1862, 12 pp. 8vo.
> Biglow Papers, second series, II.

Massinger and Ford.
> Harper's Magazine, November, 1892, v. 85, p. 942.
> The Old English Dramatists, 1892.

Masson's "Life of John Milton."
> North American Review, January, 1872, v. 114, p. 214.
> Among my Books, second series, 1876.

McClellan or Lincoln?
> North American Review, October, 1864, v. 99, p. 557.
> [The Next General Election.]
> Political Essays, 1888.

MELIBOEUS-HIPPONAX: THE BIGLOW PAPERS.
> Boston, 1848, 1867.

Memoir of Theophilus Parsons, by his Son.
> Atlantic Monthly, July, 1859, v. 4, p. 132.

Memoriae Positum. R. G. Shaw.
> Atlantic Monthly, January, 1864, v. 13, p. 88.
> Under the Willows and Other Poems, 1868.

MEMORIAL VERSES.
> Group selected from previous editions and added to Poetical
> Works, 1858.

Mercedes, 26th June, 1878.
> Harper's Magazine, January, 1881, v. 62, p. 250.

Merry England.
> Graham's Magazine, November, 1841, v. 19, p. 238.

Message of Jeff Davis in Secret Session, A.
> Atlantic Monthly, April, 1862, v. 9, p. 512.
> Biglow Papers, second series, IV.

Midnight.
> Poems, 1844.
> [Earlier Poems, 1877.]

Mill, The.

    Anti-Slavery Standard, January 4, 1849.
    Poems, v. 2, 1849. [Beaver Brook.]

Milton.

    Among My Books, second series, 1876.

Milton's "Areopagitica."

    Latest Literary Essays and Addresses, 1891.

Miner, The.

    Atlantic Monthly, August, 1866, v. 18, p. 158.
    Under the Willows and Other Poems, 1868.

MISCELLANEOUS POEMS.

    Group first appearing in complete Poetical Works, 1877.

Misconception, A.

    The Nation, August 10, 1876, v. 23, p. 86.
    Heartsease and Rue, 1888.

Miss Gilbert's Career. [Holland.]

    Atlantic Monthly, January, 1861, v. 7, p. 125.

Mobs.

    Anti-Slavery Standard, June 14, 1849.
    Anti-Slavery Papers, 1902.

Moderation.

    Anti-Slavery Standard, August 9, 1849.
    Anti-Slavery Papers, 1902.

Moieties. [Campaign Epigrams.]

    The Nation, October 12, 1876, v. 23, p. 224.

Monna Lisa.

    Heartsease and Rue, 1888.

Mood, A.

    Anti-Slavery Standard, November 15, 1849. [The Lesson of the Pine.]
    Under the Willows and Other Poems, 1868.

Moon, The.

    Graham's Magazine, February, 1843, v. 22, p. 102.
    Poems, 1844.
    [Earlier Poems, 1877.]

Moosehead Journal, A. [Addressed to the Edelmann
Storg at the Bagni di Lucca.]

Putnam's Monthly, November, 1853, v. 2, p. 457.
Fireside Travels, 1864.

Moral Movement against Slavery, The.

Anti-Slavery Standard, February 22, 1849.
Anti-Slavery Papers, 1902.

Motley (a Note).

The Nation, June 7, 1877, v. 24, p. 337.

Mr. Bowen and the Christian Examiner.

Boston Daily Advertiser, December 28, 1850, January 2,
1851.

Mr. Buchanan's Administration.

Atlantic Monthly, April, 1858, v. 1, p. 754. [Lowell's from
middle of first column on p. 754.]

Mr. Calhoun's Report.

Anti-Slavery Standard, February 15, 1849.
Anti-Slavery Papers, 1902.

Mr. Clay as an Abolitionist. Second appearance in Fifty
Years.

Anti-Slavery Standard, March 22, 1849.
Anti-Slavery Papers, 1902.

Mr. Emerson's New Course of Lectures.

The Nation, November 12, v. 7, p. 389.
My Study Windows, 1871. [Emerson, the Lecturer.]

Mr. Hosea Biglow's Speech in March Meeting.

Atlantic Monthly, May, 1866, v. 17, p. 635.
Biglow Papers, second series, xi.

Mr. Hosea Biglow to the Editor of the " Atlantic Monthly."

Atlantic Monthly, April, 1865, v. 15, p. 501.
Biglow Papers, second series, x.

Mr. Jarves's Collection.

Atlantic Monthly, 1860, v. 6, p. 509.

Mr. Webster's Speech.
>   Anti-Slavery Standard, March 21, 1850.
>   Anti-Slavery Papers, 1902.

Mr. Worsley's Nightmare.
>   The Nation, April 5, 1866, v. 2, p. 426.

"*Much have I mused.*"
>   A Year's Life, 1841.

Music.
>   Southern Literary Messenger, May, 1840, v. 6, p. 332.
>   A Year's Life, 1841.

My Appledore Gallery.   No. I.   August Afternoon.
>   The Crayon, January, 1855, v. 1, p. 9.

My Appledore Gallery.   No. II.   Sunset and Moonset.
>   The Crayon, January 31, 1855, v. 1, p. 73.
>   Under the Willows and Other Poems, 1868. [Pictures from
>   Appledore.]

My Brook.
>   New York Ledger, December 13, 1890. Supplement.

My Diary, North and South. [Russell.]
>   Atlantic Monthly, March, 1863, v. 11, p. 391.

"*My Father, since I love, thy presence cries.*"
>   Arcturus, May, 1842.

"*My Friend, adown life's valley.*"
>   A Year's Life, 1841.

"*My Friend, I pray thee call not this society.*"
>   Southern Literary Messenger, March, 1840, v. 6, p. 229.
>   A Year's Life, 1841. [Disappointment.]

My Garden Acquaintance.
>   My Study Windows, 1871.

"*My heart, I cannot still it.*"
>   A Masque of Poets, Boston, 1878.
>   Heartsease and Rue, 1888. [Auspex.]

My Lost Youth.
 Putnam's Monthly, August, 1855, v. 6, p. 122.

My Love.
 A Year's Life, 1841.
 [Earlier Poems, 1877.]

"My Love, I have no fear that thou shouldst die."
 Poems, 1844.
 [Earlier Poems, 1877.]

My Portrait Gallery.
 Atlantic Monthly, December, 1857, v. 1, p. 249.

Mystical Ballad, A.
 Graham's Magazine, May, 1844, v. 25, p. 214.

MY STUDY WINDOWS.
 Boston, 1871.

Nationality in Literature.
 North American Review, July, 1849, v. 69, p. 196.

Nest, The.
 Atlantic Monthly, March, 1858, v. 1, p. 523.
 Heartsease and Rue, 1888.

New and the Old, The. [Palmer.]
 Atlantic Monthly, September, 1859, v. 4, p. 383.

New England Two Centuries Ago.
 North American Review, January, 1865, v. 100, p. 161.
 Reprinted as 8vo pamphlet, 1865.
 Among My Books, 1870.

News from Paris, The.
 Anti-Slavery Standard, July 20, 1848.
 Anti-Slavery Papers, 1902.

New Tariff Bill, The.
 Atlantic Monthly, July, 1860, v. 6, p. 124.

New Timon, The.
 North American Review, April, 1847, v. 64, p. 460.

New Translations of the Writings of Miss Bremer.
North American Review, April, 1844, v. 58, p. 480.

New Year's Eve, 1844. A Fragment.
Graham's Magazine, July, 1844, v. 26, p. 15.

New Year's Eve, 1850.
Anti-Slavery Standard, January 10, 1850.
Under the Willows and Other Poems, 1868.

New Year's Greeting, The.
Heartsease and Rue, 1888.

Next General Election, The.
North American Review, October, 1864, v. 99, p. 557.
Political Essays, 1888. [McClellan or Lincoln?]

Nightingale in the Study, The.
Atlantic Monthly, September, 1867, v. 20, p. 323.
Under the Willows and Other Poems, 1868.

Nightwatches.
Atlantic Monthly, July, 1877, v. 40, p. 93.
Heartsease and Rue, 1888.

Nobler Lover, The.
Last Poems, 1895.

Nomades, The.
Under the Willows and Other Poems, 1868.

Nominations for the Presidency, The.
Anti-Slavery Standard, June 22, 1848.
Anti-Slavery Papers, 1902.

" No more but so ? "
A Year's Life, 1841.

Northern Sancho Panza and his Vicarious Cork Tree, The.
National Anti-Slavery Standard, July 18, 1850.

Notes of Travel and Study in Italy. [Norton.]
Atlantic Monthly, May, 1860, v. 5, p. 629.

" Now is always best."
Broadway Journal, January 25, 1845, p. 58.

Oak, The.
> Anti-Slavery Standard, December 31, 1846.
> Poems, second series, 1848.
> [Miscellaneous Poems, 1877.]

" O, child of Nature, O most meek and free."
> Southern Literary Messenger, June, 1840, v. 6, p. 470.
> A Year's Life, 1841.

Ode. " In the old days of awe and keen-eyed wonder."
> Boston Miscellany, February, 1842, v. 1, p. 59.
> Poems, 1844.
> [Earlier Poems, 1877.]

Ode for the Fourth of July, 1876, An.
> Atlantic Monthly, December, 1876, v. 38, p. 740.
> Three Memorial Poems, 1877.

Ode read at the One Hundredth Anniversary of the Fight at Concord Bridge, 19th April, 1875.
> Atlantic Monthly, June, 1875, v. 35, p. 730.
> Three Memorial Poems, 1876.

Ode recited at the Harvard Commemoration, July 21, 1865.
> Cambridge, privately printed, 1865. Royal 8vo, boards, paper label on front cover, gilt top, 50 copies printed for Lowell's use.
> Dedication: " To the ever sweet and shining memory of the ninety-three sons of Harvard College who have died for their country in the war of nationality."
> Atlantic Monthly, September, 1865, v. 16, p. 364.
> Harvard Memorial Biographies, v. 1, 1866.
> Under the Willows and Other Poems, 1868.
> Three Memorial Poems, 1876.

Ode to France. February, 1848.
> Anti-Slavery Standard, April 6, 1848.
> Poems, v. 2, 1849.
> [Miscellaneous Poems, 1877.]

Ode to Happiness.
> Atlantic Monthly, September, 1861, v. 8, p. 365.
> Under the Willows and Other Poems, 1868.

Ode. [*Written for the Celebration of the Introduction of the Cochituate Water into the City of Boston.*]
> Celebration of the Introduction of the Water of Cochituate Lake into the City of Boston. Boston, City Printer, 1848. [Sung by school-children.]
> Poems, v. 2, 1849.
> [Miscellaneous Poems, 1877.]

"O happy childhood."
> Poems, 1844.

Old English Dramatists, The.
> Boston Miscellany, April, May, August, 1842, v. 1, pp. 145, 201, v. 2, p. 49.
> Early Prose Writings, 1902.

Old English Dramatists, The.
> Harper's Magazine, June, 1892, v. 85, p. 75. [Introductory lecture.]
> The Old English Dramatists, 1892.
> Latest Literary Essays [added to]. Elmwood Edition.

OLD ENGLISH DRAMATISTS, THE.
> Boston, 1892.

Old Poets, The.
> Graham's Magazine, February, 1842, p. 90.

Olmstead's "A Journey in the Back Country."
> Atlantic Monthly, November, 1860.

On a Bust of General Grant.
> Scribner's Magazine, March, 1892, v. 11, p. 267.
> Last Poems, 1895.

On a Certain Condescension in Foreigners.
> Atlantic Monthly, January, 1869, v. 23, p. 82.
> My Study Windows, 1871.

On a Portrait of Dante by Giotto.
> Poems, second series, 1848.
> [Miscellaneous Poems, 1877.]

On an Autumn Sketch of H. G. Wild.
> Heartsease and Rue, 1888.

On being asked for an Autograph in Venice.
 Atlantic Monthly, July, 1875, v. 36, p. 37.
 Heartsease and Rue, 1888.

On Board the '76. [*Written for Mr. Bryant's Seventieth Birthday, November 3, 1864.*]
 Atlantic Monthly, January, 1865, v. 15, p. 107.
 Under the Willows and Other Poems, 1868.

On Burning some Old Letters.
 Heartsease and Rue, 1888.

One Great Lesson, The.
 The Liberty Bell, 1842. [No. ii of "Sonnets."]

On Hearing a Sonata of Beethoven's played in the Next Room.
 Last Poems, 1895.

"Only as thou herein canst not see me."
 The Dial, January, 1842, p. 357.

"Only full obedience is free."
 Anti-Slavery Standard, January 27, 1842.

On my Twenty-fourth Birth-day, February 22, 1843.
 Poems, 1844.

On Planting a Tree at Inveraray.
 Heartsease and Rue, 1888.

On reading Spenser again.
 A Year's Life, 1841.

On reading Wordsworth's Sonnets in Defence of Capital Punishment.
 Democratic Review, May, 1842, v. 10, p. 479.
 Poems, 1844.
 [Earlier Poems, 1877.]

On receiving a Copy of Mr. Austin Dobson's "Old World Idylls."
 Heartsease and Rue, 1888.

On receiving a Piece of Flax-cotton.
 Anti-Slavery Standard, May 1, 1851.

On the Capture of certain Fugitive Slaves near Washington.
>   Boston Courier, July 19, 1845.
>   Poems, second series, 1848.
>   [Miscellaneous Poems, 1877.]

On the Death of a Friend's Child.
>   Democratic Review, October, 1844, v. 15, p. 377.
>   Poems, second series, 1848.
>   [Miscellaneous Poems, 1877.]

On the Death of Charles Turner Torrey.
>   Poems, second series, 1848.
>   [Memorial Verses, 1877.]

On Translating Homer. [Arnold.]
>   Atlantic Monthly, January, 1862, v. 9, p. 142.

Optimist, The.
>   Heartsease and Rue, 1888.

Oriental Apologue, An.
>   Anti-Slavery Standard, April 12, 1849.
>   Poetical Works, 1877.

Origin of Didactic Poetry, The.
>   Atlantic Monthly, November, 1857, v. 1, p. 110.
>   Heartsease and Rue, 1888.

Orpheus.
>   The American Review, August, 1845, v. 2, p. 131.

"Our Literature."
>   Literary and Political Addresses, 1904.

"*Our love is not a fading earthly flower.*"
>   Poems, 1844.
>   [Earlier Poems, 1877.]

Our Own: His Wanderings and Adventures.
>   Putnam's Monthly, April, May, June, 1853, v. 1, pp. 406, 533, 687.

Our Position.
    Pennsylvania Freeman, January 16, 1844.
Our Southern Brethren.
    Anti-Slavery Standard, January, 1849.
    Anti-Slavery Papers, 1902.
Out of Doors.
    Graham's Magazine, April, 1850, v. 36, p. 257.
Palfrey's "History of New England."
    North American Review, January, 1865, v. 100, p. 161.
Palinode. [Autumn.]
    Putnam's Monthly, December, 1854, v. 4, p. 570.
    Second part of "Auf Wiedersehen."
    Under the Willows and Other Poems, 1868.
Palmer's "Folk-Songs."
    Atlantic Monthly, December, 1860, v. 6, p. 761.
Palmer's "The New and the Old."
    Atlantic Monthly, September, 1859.
Paola to Francesca.
    Heartsease and Rue, 1888.
Parable, A.
    Heartsease and Rue, 1888.
Parable, A. "Said Christ our Lord."
    Anti-Slavery Standard, May 18, 1848.
    Poems, v. 2, 1849.
    [Miscellaneous Poems, 1877.]
Parable, A. "Worn and foot-sore was the prophet."
    Democratic Review, February, 1843, v. 12, p. 145.
    Poems, 1844.
    [Earlier Poems, 1877.]
Parkman's "France and England."
    North American Review, October, 1865, v. 101, p. 625.
Parkman's "France and England in North America."
    North American Review, July, 1867, v. 105, p. 321.

Parting of the Ways, The.
> Anti-Slavery Standard, February 8, 1848.
> Under the Willows and Other Poems, 1868.

Peck's "Forty Years of Pioneer Life."
> North American Review, October, 1864, v. 99, p. 627.

Pennsylvania Academy of Fine Arts, The.
> Broadway Journal, February 22, 1845.

Peschiera.
> Putnam's Monthly, May, 1854, v. 2, p. 522.

Pessimoptimism.
> Heartsease and Rue, 1888.

Petition, The.
> Heartsease and Rue, 1888.

Phœbe.
> Century, November, 1881, v. 23, p. 90.
> Heartsease and Rue, 1888.

Pickens-and-Stealin's Rebellion, The.
> Atlantic Monthly, June, 1861, v. 7, p. 757.
> Political Essays, 1888.

Pictures from Appledore.
> I–IV, August Afternoon, The Crayon, January 3, 1855.
> V, Appledore, Graham's Magazine, February, 1851, v. 37, p. 87.
> VI, Sunset and Moonset, The Crayon, January 31, 1855.
> Under the Willows and Other Poems, 1868.

Pioneer, The.
> Poems, second series, 1848.
> [Miscellaneous Poems, 1877.]

Pious Editor's Creed, The.
> Anti-Slavery Standard, May 4, 1848.
> Biglow Papers, first series, VI.

Place of the Independent in Politics, The.
> Address to Reform Club, New York, April 13, 1888.
> Reform Club Series, No. I, New York, Reform Club, 1888.
> Political Essays, 1888.

Plays of Thomas Middleton, The.
>The Pioneer, January, 1843.
>Early Prose Writings, 1902.

Plea for Freedom from Speech and Figures of Speech-Makers, A.
>Atlantic Monthly, December, 1860, v. 6, p. 740.

Pocket Celebration of the Fourth, The.
>Atlantic Monthly, August, 1858, v. 2, p. 374.

Poems. [Rose Terry.]
>Atlantic Monthly, March, 1861, v. 7, p. 382.

Poems by John James Piatt.
>North American Review, October, 1868, v. 101, p. 660.

Poems by Two Friends.
>Atlantic Monthly, April, 1860, v. 5, p. 510.

Poems of Robert Lowell, The.
>North American Review, April, 1864, v. 98, p. 617.

POEMS OF THE WAR.
>Under the Willows and Other Poems, 1868.
>[Poetical Works, 1877.]

Poet, The.
>A Year's Life, 1841.

Poet, The.
>Arcturus, February, 1842, p. 201.
>Poems, 1844.

"Poet, if men from wisdom turn away."
>Anti-Slavery Standard, September 1, 1842.

"Poet, who sittest in thy pleasant room."
>A Year's Life, 1841.

POLITICAL ESSAYS.
>Boston, 1888.

Politics and the Pulpit.
>Anti-Slavery Standard, January 25, 1849.
>Anti-Slavery Papers, 1902.

Pope.
> North American Review, January, 1871, v. 112, p. 178.
> My Study Windows, 1871.

POWER OF SOUND, THE: A RHYMED LECTURE.
> Privately printed, New York, 1896.

Prayer, A.
> Poems, 1844.
> [Earlier Poems, 1877.]

Pregnant Comment, The.
> Heartsease and Rue, 1888.

Prejudice of Color, The.
> Pennsylvania Freeman, February 13, 1845.
> Anti-Slavery Papers, 1902.

Present Crisis, The. [December, 1844.]
> Boston Courier, December 11, 1845. [Verses suggested by the Present Crisis.]
> Poems, second series, 1848.
> [Miscellaneous Poems, 1877.]

President on the Stump, The.
> North American Review, April, 1866, v. 102, p. 530.
> Political Essays, 1888.

Presidential Candidates.
> Anti-Slavery Standard, May 11, 1848.
> Anti-Slavery Papers, 1902.

President's Message, The.
> Anti-Slavery Standard, December 14, 1848.
> Anti-Slavery Papers, 1902.

President's Policy, The.
> North American Review, January, 1864, v. 98, p. 234.

President Tyler's Message on the African Slave Trade.
> Pennsylvania Freeman, March 13, 1844.

Prior's "Ancient Danish Ballads."
> Atlantic Monthly, January, 1861, v. 7, p. 124.

Prison of Cervantes, The.
> Harper's Magazine, January, 1881, v. 62, p. 250.
> Heartsease and Rue, 1888.

Progress of the World, The.
> Introduction to The World's Progress, Boston, 1886.
> Latest Literary Essays, 1891.

Prometheus.
> Democratic Review, August, 1843, v. 13, p. 147.
> Poems, 1844.
> [Miscellaneous Poems, 1877.]

Pro-Slavery Logic.
> Anti-Slavery Standard, November 23, 1848.
> Anti-Slavery Papers, 1902.

Protest, The.
> Heartsease and Rue, 1888.

Pseudo-Conservatism.
> Anti-Slavery Standard, November 14, 1850.
> Anti-Slavery Papers, 1902.

Public Opinion.
> Anti-Slavery Standard, May 10, 1849.
> Anti-Slavery Papers, 1902.

Putting the Cart before the Horse.
> Anti-Slavery Standard, October 4, 1849.
> Anti-Slavery Papers, 1902.

Question of the Hour, The.
> Atlantic Monthly, January, 1861, v. 7, p. 117.

Rallying Cry for New England against the Annexation of Texas, by a Yankee, A.
> Boston Courier, March 19, 1844.
> Harper's Weekly, April 23, 1892, v. 36, p. 393.

Reading.
> A Year's Life, 1841.

Rebellion; its Causes and Consequences, The.
> North American Review, July, 1864, v. 99, p. 246.
> Political Essays, 1888.

Recall, The.
>Heartsease and Rue, 1888.

Reconstruction.
>North American Review, April, 1865, v. 100, p. 540.
>Political Essays, 1888.

Red Tape.
>A Masque of Poets, Boston, 1878.
>Heartsease and Rue, 1888. [The Brakes.]

Reform.
>Arcturus, February, 1842, p. 200.
>Poems, 1844.

Reform.
>Poems, v. 1, 1849.

Remarks of Increase D. O'Phace, Esq.
>Boston Courier, December 28, 1847.
>Biglow Papers, first series, IV.

Remembered Music. A Fragment.
>Broadway Journal, February 15, 1844.
>Poems, second series, 1848.
>[Earlier Poems, 1877.]

Reply to the "Statement of the Trustees" of the Dudley Observatory.
>Atlantic Monthly, November, 1859, v. 4, p. 650.

Requiem, A.
>The Gift; a Christmas and New Year's Present, Philadelphia, 1844.
>Poems, 1844.
>[Earlier Poems, 1877.]

Restaurant, The.
>Putnam's Monthly, May, 1854, v. 3, p. 559.   No. II in "Without and Within."

Reverie, A.
>Graham's Magazine, October, 1843, v. 24, p. 183
>Poems, 1844.

Review of the Works of John Webster.
>   Atlantic Monthly, June, 1858, v. 2, p. 119.

Rhœcus.
>   Poems, 1844.
>   [Miscellaneous Poems, 1877.]

" Richard III."
>   Latest Literary Essays, 1891.

Roba di Roma. [Story.]
>   Atlantic Monthly, April, 1863, v. 11, p. 515.

Roman Republic, The.
>   Anti-Slavery Standard, July 12, 1849.
>   Anti-Slavery Papers, 1902.

Rosaline.
>   Graham's Magazine, February, 1842, v. 20, p. 89.
>   Poems, v. 1, 1849.
>   [Earlier Poems, 1877.]

Rose. [Sonnets on Names.]
>   A Year's Life, 1841.

Rose, The.
>   The Pioneer, January, 1843.

Rose, The: A Ballad.
>   Poems, 1844.
>   [Earlier Poems, 1877.]

Round Table, The.
>   Atlantic Monthly, November, 1857, v. 1, p. 121.

Rousseau and the Sentimentalists.
>   North American Review, July, 1867, v. 105, p. 242.
>   Among My Books, first series, 1870.

Royal Pedigree, The.
>   Anti-Slavery Standard, August 20, 1846.
>   Boston Courier, December 4, 1846.
>   Poems, second series, 1848.

Sacred Parasol, The.
>   Anti-Slavery Standard, June 8, 1848.
>   Anti-Slavery Papers, 1902.

St. Michael the Weigher.
>Last Poems, 1895.

Sample of Consistency, A.
>Atlantic Monthly, November, 1858, v. 2, p. 750.

Sapphire.
>The Ladies' Casket, Lowell, 1846.

"Sayest thou, most beautiful."
>A Year's Life, 1841.

Sayings. .
>Heartsease and Rue, 1888.

Scherzo.
>Heartsease and Rue, 1888.

Science and Poetry.
>Heartsease and Rue, 1888.

Scotch the Snake or Kill it?
>North American Review, July, 1865, v. 101, p. 190.
>Political Essays, 1888.

Scottish Border.
>Atlantic Monthly, July, 1875, v. 36, p. 37. [Sonnets from
>Over Sea, i, English Border.]
>Heartsease and Rue, 1888.

Search, The.
>Anti-Slavery Standard, February 25, 1847.
>Poems, second series, 1848.
>[Miscellaneous Poems, 1877.]

Seaweed.
>Gifts of Genius; a Miscellany, 1859.
>Under the Willows and Other Poems, 1868.

Second Letter from B. Sawin, Esq.
>Anti-Slavery Standard, July 6, 1848.
>Biglow Papers, first series, viii.

Secret, The.
>Atlantic Monthly, January, 1888, v. 61, p. 95.
>Heartsease and Rue, 1888.

Self-Possession *vs.* Prepossession.
> Atlantic Monthly, December, 1861, v. 8, p. 761.

Self-Study.
> ' Under the Willows and Other Poems, 1868.

Serenade. "From the close-shut window gleams no spark."
> A Year's Life, 1841.
> Poems, v. 1, 1849.
> [Earlier Poems, 1877.]

Serenade, The. "Gentle, Lady, be thy sleeping."
> Southern Literary Messenger, April, 1840, p. 248.
> A Year's Life, 1841.

Seward-Johnson Reaction, The.
> North American Review, October, 1866, v. 103, p. 520.
> Political Essays, 1888.

Shadow of Dante, The.
> North American Review, July, 1872, v. 115, p. 139.
> Among My Books, second series, 1876. [Dante.]

Shakespeare Once More.
> North American Review, April, 1868, v. 106, p. 629.
> Among My Books, first series, 1870.
> Essays from the North American Review, edited by Allen Thorndike Rice. New York, Appletons, 1879.

Shakespeare's "Richard III."
> Address before the Edinburgh Philosophical Institution, 1883.
> Atlantic Monthly, December, 1891, v. 68, p. 816.
> Latest Literary Essays and Addresses, 1892.
> [Literary and Political Addresses, 1904.]

Shall we ever be Republican ?
> Anti-Slavery Standard, April 20, 1848.
> Anti-Slavery Papers, 1902.

She came and went.
> Poems, v. 2, 1849.
> [Miscellaneous Poems, 1877.]

Shelley.
> Introduction to Poetical Works of Shelley, Boston, 1857.

Shepherd of King Admetus, The.
>   Boston Miscellany, September, 1842, v. 2, p. 138.
>   Poems, 1844.
>   [Miscellaneous Poems, 1877.]

Shipwreck.
>   Atlantic Monthly, June, 1858, v. 2, p. 101.

Si descendero in Infernum, ades.
>   The Harbinger, January 16, 1847, v. 4, p. 94.
>   Poems, second series, 1848.
>   [Miscellaneous Poems, 1877.]

Silence.
>   Poems, 1844.

" Silent as one who treads."
>   A Year's Life, 1841.

Singing Leaves, The: A Ballad.
>   Graham's Magazine, January, 1854.
>   Under the Willows and Other Poems, 1868.

Singing to the Eternal Ear.
>   National Anti-Slavery Standard, September, 1842.

"Sir Rohan's Ghost."
>   Atlantic Monthly, February, 1860, v. 5, p. 252.

Sirens, The.
>   A Year's Life, 1841.
>   [Earlier Poems, 1877.]

Sixty-Eighth Birthday.
>   Heartsease and Rue, 1888.

Skillygoliana.
>   Harvardiana, February, 1838, p. 196.

Slaveholding Territories.
>   Anti-Slavery Standard, April 19, 1849.
>   Anti-Slavery Papers, 1902.

" Slow opening flower."
>   Poems, 1844.

Some Letters of Walter Savage Landor.
>Century, February, 1888, v. 35, p. 511.
>Latest Literary Essays, 1891.

Something Natural.
>A Year's Life, 1841.

Song. "A pair of black eyes."
>Harvardiana, July, 1838, p. 389.

Song. "Lift up the curtains of thine eyes."
>Southern Literary Messenger, June, 1840, v. 6, p. 416.
>A Year's Life, 1841.

Song. "O moonlight deep and tender."
>Poems, 1844.
>[Earlier Poems, 1877.]

Song. "Oh! I must look on that sweet face once more before I die."
>Southern Literary Messenger, June, 1840, p. 414.
>A Year's Life, 1841.

Song. "There is a light in thy blue eyes."
>Poems, 1844.

Song. To M. L.
>Poems, second series, 1848.
>[Earlier Poems, 1877.]

Song to my Wife, A.
>Broadway Journal, January 4, 1845.

Song. "Violet! sweet violet."
>Poems, 1844.
>[Earlier Poems, 1877.]

Song. "What reck I of the stars when I."
>Southern Literary Messenger, March, 1840, v. 6, p. 213.
>A Year's Life, 1841.

Song-Writing.
>The Pioneer, February, 1843.
>Early Prose Writings, 1902.

Sonnet. On being asked for an Autograph in Venice.
> Atlantic Monthly, July, 1875, v. 36, p. 37. [Sonnets from
> Over Sea, II.]
> Heartsease and Rue, 1888.

Sonnet. To Fanny Alexander.
> Atlantic Monthly, May, 1875, v. 35, p. 560.
> Heartsease and Rue, 1888.

Sonnet to Keats.
> Boston Miscellany, January, 1842, v. 1, p. 3.

Sonnets from Over Sea.
> Atlantic Monthly, July, 1875, v. 36, p. 37.
> Heartsease and Rue, 1888. [Scottish Border. On being asked
> for an Autograph in Venice.]

Sonnets on Names.
> A Year's Life, 1841.

South as King Log, The.
> Anti-Slavery Standard, February 21, 1850.
> Anti-Slavery Papers, 1902.

Sower, The.
> Poems, v. 2, 1849.
> [Miscellaneous Poems, 1877.]

Speech of Honble Preserved Doe in Secret Caucus.
> Atlantic Monthly, May, 1862, v. 9, p. 841.
> Biglow Papers, second series, v.

Spenser.
> North American Review, April, 1875, v. 120, p. 334.
> Among My Books, second series, 1876.

Sphinx.
> A Year's Life, 1841.

Stanley.
> Speech in Westminster Abbey, December 13, 1881.
> Democracy and Other Addresses, 1886.

Stanzas on Freedom.
> Poems, 1844. [Stanzas sung at the Anti-Slavery Picnic

in Dedham on the Anniversary of West-Indian Emancipation, August 1, 1843.]
[Miscellaneous Poems, 1877.]

Stedman's "Alice of Monmouth."
North American Review, January, 1864, v. 98, p. 292.

Street, The.
The Pioneer, March, 1843.
Poems, 1844.
[Earlier Poems, 1877.]

Studies for Two Heads.
Poems, second series, 1848.
[Miscellaneous Poems, 1877.]

Study for a Head.
The Young American's Magazine, July, 1847, v. 1, p. 268.
Poems, second series, 1848.
[Miscellaneous Poems, 1877.] [First part of "Studies for Two Heads."]

Study of Modern Languages, The.
Address before Modern Language Association, 1889.
Latest Literary Essays and Addresses, 1891.

Sub Pondere crescit.
Arcturus, May, 1842.
Poems, 1844.
[Earlier Poems, 1877.]

Summer Storm.
Poems, second series, 1848.
[Earlier Poems, 1877.]

Sun-Worship.
Heartsease and Rue, 1888.

Sunset and Moonset.
The Crayon, January 31, 1855.
Pictures from Appledore, vi.

Sunset and Moonshine.
Arcturus, January, 1842, p. 141.

Sunthin' in the Pastoral Line.
> Atlantic Monthly, June, 1862, v. 9, p. 790.
> Biglow Papers, second series, VI.

Swinburne's Tragedies.
> North American Review, April, 1866, v. 102, p. 544.
> My Study Windows, 1871.

Sympathy with Ireland.
> Anti-Slavery Standard, June 29, 1848.
> Anti-Slavery Papers, 1902.

Tariff Reform.
> Address at Tariff Reform League, Boston, 1887.
> Literary and Political Addresses, 1904.

Telepathy.
> Heartsease and Rue, 1888.

Tempora Mutantur.
> The Nation, August 26, 1875, v. 21, p. 130.
> Heartsease and Rue, 1888.

Ten Years of Preacher-Life. [Milburn.]
> Atlantic Monthly, December, 1859, v. 4, p. 770.

Tennyson's "Enoch Arden."
> North American Review, October, 1864, v. 99, p. 626.

Tennyson's "Princess."
> Massachusetts Quarterly Review, March, 1848.

Texas.
> Pennsylvania Freeman, January 30, 1845.
> Anti-Slavery Papers, 1902.

Thackeray's "Roundabout Papers."
> North American Review, April, 1864, v. 98, p. 624.

Thankfulness.
> Poems, 1844.

" The gentle Una I have loved."
> A Year's Life, 1841. [Dedication.]

" *The hungry flame did never yet seem hot.*"
>The Liberty Bell, 1842.
>Poems, 1844. [The Fiery Trial.]

" *The Maple puts her corals on in May.*"
>Atlantic Monthly, November, 1857, v. 1, p. 120.
>Heartsease and Rue, 1888. [The Maple.]

" *The Soul would fain.*"
>A Year's Life, 1841.

" *There never yet was flower fair in vain.*"
>Poems, 1844.
>[Earlier Poems, 1877.]

" *Therefore think not the Past is wise alone.*"
>The Present, April 1, 1844, p. 425.

Third Letter from B. Sawin, Esq., A.
>Biglow Papers, second series, ix.

Thistle-downs.
>Poems, v. 1, 1849.

Thoreau Letters.
>North American Review, October, 1865, v. 101, p. 397.
>My Study Windows, 1871. [Thoreau.]

Thoreau's "Week."
>Massachusetts Quarterly Review, December, 1849, v. 3,
>   p. 40.

" *Thou art a woman.*"
>Anti-Slavery Standard, February 3, 1842.

Three Memorial Poems.
>Boston, 1877.

Threnodia on an Infant.
>Knickerbocker Magazine, May, 1839.
>A Year's Life, 1841. [Threnodia.]
>[Earlier Poems, 1877.]

To ——.
>A Year's Life, 1841.

To ——, after a Snow-storm.
  A Year's Life, 1841.

To ——. "We, too, have autumns, when our leaves."
  Anti-Slavery Standard, October 18, 1849.
  Poems, v. 2, 1849.
  [Miscellaneous Poems, 1877.]

To A. C. L. [Mrs. Anna Cabot Lowell.]
  Poems, 1844.
  [Earlier Poems, 1877.]

To a Friend.
  A Year's Life, 1841.

To a Friend who gave me a group of weeds and grasses.
  The Mercantile, Boston, March 21, 1875; in connection with
    Fair in aid of Mercantile Library Association.
  Heartsease and Rue, 1888.

To a Friend who sent me a Meerschaum.
  Spirit of the Fair, New York, April 12, 1864, p. 79. [For
    "Metropolitan Fair" of Sanitary Commission.]
  Heartsease and Rue, 1888. [To C. F. Bradford.]

To a Lady playing on the Cithern.
  Heartsease and Rue, 1888.

To a Pine Tree.
  The Harbinger, August 2, 1845, v. 1, p. 122.
  Poems, second series, 1848.
  [Miscellaneous Poems, 1877.]

To a Voice heard in Mount Auburn, July, 1839.
  The Dial, January, 1841, p. 366.
  A Year's Life, 1841.

To an Æolian Harp at Night.
  Boston Miscellany, December, 1842, v. 2, p. 267.

To C. F. Bradford, on the Gift of a Meerschaum Pipe.
  Spirit of the Fair, April 12, 1864.
  Heartsease and Rue, 1888.

To Charles Eliot Norton. [*Agro Dolce.*]
Under the Willows and Other Poems, 1868.

To Cuba and Back. [Dana.]
Atlantic Monthly, July, 1859, v. 4, p. 132.

"*To die is gain.*"
The Dial, July, 1841, p. 129.

To E. W. G. [E. W. Gilman.]
A Year's Life, 1841.

To Holmes on his Seventieth Birthday.
Heartsease and Rue, 1888.

To H. W. L., on his Birthday, 27th February, 1867.
Under the Willows and Other Poems, 1868.

To Irene on her Birthday.
The Dial, January, 1842, p. 358.

To John Gorham Palfrey.
Anti-Slavery Standard, November 2, 1848.
Poems, v. 2, 1849.
[Memorial Verses, 1858.]

To J. R. Giddings.
Poems, 1844.
[Earlier Poems, 1877.]

To Lamartine.
Anti-Slavery Standard, August 3, 1848.
Poems, v. 2, 1849.
[Memorial Verses, 1858.]

To Miss D. T. on her giving me a drawing of little Street Arabs.
Heartsease and Rue, 1888.

To M. O. S.
The Pioneer, February, 1843. [To —— "Mary, since first I knew thee."]
Poems, 1844.
[Earlier Poems, 1877.]

To Mount Washington, on a Second Visit.
    Harvardiana, July, 1838, p. 387.

To Mr. John Bartlett, who had sent me a seven-pound trout.
    Atlantic Monthly, July, 1866, v. 18, p. 47.
    With Bartlett's Catalogue of Books on Angling, Cambridge,
        1882; inserted.
    Under the Willows and Other Poems, 1868.

To M. W., on her Birthday.
    Poems, 1844. [To ——, on her Birthday.]
    [Earlier Poems, 1877.]

To Perdita, singing.
    Boston Miscellany, January, 1842, v. 1, p. 23.
    Poems, 1844.
    [Earlier Poems, 1877.]

To the Dandelion.
    Graham's Magazine, January, 1845, v. 27, p. 4.
    Poems, second series, 1848.
    [Miscellaneous Poems, 1877.]

" To the dark, narrow house."
    A Year's Life, 1841.

To the Evening Star.
    A Year's Life, 1841.

To the Future.
    Graham's Magazine, August, 1845, v. 28, p. 52.
    Poems, second series, 1848.
    [Miscellaneous Poems, 1877.]

To the Memory of Hood.
    Anti-Slavery Standard, September 21, 1848.
    Poems, v. 1, 1849.
    [Memorial Verses, 1858.]

To the Muse.
    Under the Willows and Other Poems, 1868.

To the Past.
    Graham's Magazine, January, 1846, v. 28, p. 39.
    Poems, second series, 1848.
    [Miscellaneous Poems, 1877.]

To the Spirit of Keats.
> Arcturus, January, 1842.
> Poems, 1844.
> [Earlier Poems, 1877.]

To Whittier, on his Seventy-fifth Birthday.
> Heartsease and Rue, 1888.

To W. L. Garrison.
> Anti-Slavery Standard, October 16, 1848.   [The Day of
>   Small Things.]
> Poems, v. 2, 1849.
> [Memorial Verses, 1858.]

Token, The.
> Poems, 1844.
> [Earlier Poems, 1877.]

Trial.
> Anti-Slavery Standard, June 28, 1849. [Two Sonnets.]
> Poems, v. 1, 1849.
> [Miscellaneous Poems, 1877.]

Tribute to C. F. Adams.
> Proceedings Massachusetts Historical Society, 1887.

Tribute to John P. Kennedy.
> Proceedings Massachusetts Historical Society, 1870.

Tribute to Edmund Quincy.
> Proceedings Massachusetts Historical Society, 1877.

Trowbridge's "Old Battle-Ground."
> Atlantic Monthly, September, 1860, v. 6, p. 376.

Trübner's Bibliographical Guide to American Literature.
> Atlantic Monthly, June, 1859, v. 3, p. 777.

True Radical, The.
> Boston Miscellany, July, 1842, v. 2, p. 77.

Trustee's Lament, The.
> Atlantic Monthly, August, 1858, v. 2, p. 370.

Tuckerman's "America and its Commentators."
> North American Review, October, 1864, v. 99, p. 624.

Turkish Tyranny and American.
>Anti-Slavery Standard, December 13, 1849.
>Anti-Slavery Papers, 1902.

Turncoats.
>Anti-Slavery Standard, September 14, 1848.
>Anti-Slavery Papers, 1902.

Turner's Old Téméraire: Under a Figure symbolizing the Church.
>Atlantic Monthly, April, 1888, v. 61, p. 482.
>Last Poems, 1895.

Two, The.
>Boston Miscellany, May, 1842, v. 1, p. 213.

Two Gunners, The: A Fable.
>Biglow Papers, first series, Introduction.

Two Scenes from the Life of Blondel. Autumn, 1863.
>Atlantic Monthly, November, 1863, v. 12, p. 576.
>Under the Willows and Other Poems, 1868.

[Two Sonnets to Wordsworth.]
>Graham's Magazine, March, 1843, v. 22, p. 190.

Uncle Cobus's Story.
>Our Young Folks, July, 1866.

Under the October Maples.
>Heartsease and Rue, 1888.

Under the Old Elm. [Poem read at Cambridge on the hundredth anniversary of Washington's taking command of the American Army, 3d July, 1775.]
>Atlantic Monthly, August, 1875, v. 36, p. 221. [Under the Great Elm.]
>Cambridge in the Centennial Proceedings, Cambridge, 1875.
>Three Memorial Poems, 1876.

UNDER THE WILLOWS.
>Atlantic Monthly, June, 1868, v. 21, p. 754. [A June Idyll.]
>Under the Willows and Other Poems, 1868.

Unhappy Lot of Mr. Knott, The.
> Graham's Magazine, April, 1851, v. 38, p. 281.
> Poetical Works, 1869.

Union, The.
> Pennsylvania Freeman, April 10, 1845.

Unlovely, The.
> A Year's Life, 1841.

Up and Down the Irriwadi. [Palmer.]
> Atlantic Monthly, September, 1859, v. 4, p. 383.

Valentine, A.
> Last Poems, 1895.

"Verse cannot tell how beautiful thou art."
> Southern Literary Messenger, March, 1840, v. 6, p. 207.
> A Year's Life, 1841.

Verses, intended to go with a Posset Dish.
> Last Poems, 1895.

Verses suggested by the Present Crisis.
> Boston Courier, December 11, 1845.
> Poems, second series, 1848. [The Present Crisis.]
> [Miscellaneous Poems, 1877.]

Villa Franca, 1859.
> Atlantic Monthly, December, 1859, v. 4, p. 738. [Italy.]
> Under the Willows and Other Poems, 1868.

"Violet ! sweet violet !"
> Graham's Magazine, January, 1842, v. 20, p. 37.
> Poems, 1844.
> [Earlier Poems, 1877.]

Virginian in New England Thirty-five Years Ago, A.
> Atlantic Monthly, August, 1870, v. 26, p. 162. [Introduction
> to Diary of Lucian Minor of Virginia, 1834, which ap-
> peared in September, October, December, 1870, and June,
> 1871.]

VISION OF SIR LAUNFAL, THE.
> Cambridge, 1848.

Voltaire.
> The Pioneer, January, 1843.

Voyage down the Amoor, A. [Collins.]
> Atlantic Monthly, June, 1860, v. 5, p. 757.

Voyage to Vineland, The.
> Under the Willows and Other Poems, 1868.

Walton.
> The Nation, April 27, 1876, v. 22, p. 283.
> Introduction to John Bartlett's ed. of "Complete Angler," 1889.
> Latest Literary Essays and Addresses, 1891.

Washers of the Shroud, The. October, 1861.
> Atlantic Monthly, November, 1861, v. 8, p. 641.
> Under the Willows and Other Poems, 1868.

Washington Monument, A.
> Anti-Slavery Standard, December 28, 1848.
> Anti-Slavery Papers, 1902.

Webster [John].
> Harper's Magazine, August, 1892, v. 85, p. 411.
> The Old English Dramatists, 1904.

Webster's Dictionary.
> North American Review, January, 1865, v. 100, p. 299.

Wendell Phillips.
> Poems, 1844.
> [Earlier Poems, 1877.]

Wendell Phillips in Congress.
> The Nation, October 4, 1866, v. 3, p. 272.

What is it ?
> Harvardiana, October, 1837, v. 4, p. 57.

What Mr. Robinson thinks.
> Boston Courier, November 2, 1847.
> Biglow Papers, first series, iii.

What Rabbi Jehosha Said. [Originally written for a Fair in St. Louis.]
> The Nation, January 18, 1866, v. 2, p. 72.
> Under the Willows and Other Poems, 1868.

"What reck I of the stars when I."
> Southern Literary Messenger, March, 1840, v. 6, p. 213.

What shall be done for the Hungarian Exiles?
> Boston Courier, January 3, 1850.

"What were I, Love?"
> Poems, 1844.
> [Earlier Poems, 1877.]

What will Mr. Webster do?
> Anti-Slavery Standard, July 13, 1848.
> Anti-Slavery Papers, 1902.

"When in a book I find a pleasant thought."
> The Dial, January, 1842, p. 357.

"When the glad soul is full."
> A Year's Life, 1841.

"Whene'er I read in mournful history."
> Boston Miscellany, May, 1842, v. 1, p. 200.

White's Shakespeare.
> Atlantic Monthly, January, February, 1859, v. 3, pp. 111, 241.

Whittier's "Home Ballads and Poems."
> Atlantic Monthly, November, 1860, v. 6, p. 637.

Whittier's "In War Time."
> North American Review, January, 1864, v. 98, p. 290.

Whittier's Poems.
> Anti-Slavery Standard, December 14, 1848.

Whittier's "Snow-Bound."
> North American Review, April, 1866, v. 102, p. 631.

"Why should we ever weary of this life ?"
A Year's Life, 1841.

Widow's Mite, The. [Campaign Epigrams.]
The Nation, September 14, 1876, v. 23, p. 163.

Windharp, The.
Putnam's Monthly, December, 1854, v. 4, p. 569.
Under the Willows and Other Poems, 1868.

Winter.
The Present, March 1, 1844.

Winter Evening Hymn to my Fire, A.
Putnam's Monthly, March, 1854, v. 3, p. 328.
Under the Willows and Other Poems, 1868.

Winthrop Papers, The.
North American Review, October, 1867, v. 105, p. 592.

Witchcraft.
North American Review, January, 1868, v. 106, pp. 176, 232.
Reprinted as pamphlet, 1868.
Among My Books, first series, 1870.

With a Copy of Aucassin and Nicolete.
Heartsease and Rue, 1888.

With a Pair of Gloves lost in a Wager.
Heartsease and Rue, 1888.

With a Pressed Flower.
Poems, v. 1, 1849.
[Earlier Poems, 1877.]

With a Seashell.
Heartsease and Rue, 1888.

With an Armchair.
Heartsease and Rue, 1888.

Without and Within.
Putnam's Magazine, April, 1854, v. 3, p. 426.
Under the Willows and Other Poems, 1868.

Woman.
> Boston Miscellany, May, 1842, p. 200.

Word in Season, A.
> Pennsylvania Freeman, January 16, 1845.
> Anti-Slavery Papers, 1902.

Wordsworth.
> Introduction to Wordsworth's Poetical Works, Boston, 1854.
> Among My Books, second series, 1876.

Wordsworth. [Address as President of the Wordsworth Society, May 10, 1884.]
> Democracy and Other Addresses, 1886.

Works of Edmund Burke, The.
> North American Review, April, 1866, v. 102, p. 634.

Works of Walter Savage Landor, The.
> Massachusetts Quarterly Review, December, 1848.

World's Fair, The. 1876.
> The Nation, August 5, 1875, v. 21, p. 82.

Worthy Ditty, A.
> The Nation, January, 1866, p. 106.

" Ye who behold the body of my thought."
> Poems, 1844.

Ye Yankees of the Bay State.
> Boston Morning Post, February 26, 1839.

Youthful Experiment in English Hexameters, A.
> Heartsease and Rue, 1888.

Yussouf.
> The Liberty Bell, 1851.
> Under the Willows and Other Poems, 1868.

CHRONOLOGICAL LIST OF SEPARATE WORKS AND EDITIONS

HARVARDIANA

HARVARDIANA. Volume IV. Cambridge: Published by *John Owen*. MDCCCXXXVIII.

During 1837 Lowell was one of the editors of this college magazine, and his contributions were as follows:

No. I. September, 1837.
New Poem of Homer, p. 18.
Imitation of Burns (verse), p. 31.
Dramatic Sketch (verse), p. 39.

No. II. October.
A Voice from the Tombs, p. 53.
What is it? (verse), p. 57.
Hints to Theme Writers, p. 58.
Obituary, p. 64.
The Serenade (verse), p. 65.
The Old Bell, p. 74.

No. III. November.
The Idler, p. 29.
Saratoga Lake, p. 111.
Hints to Reviewers, No. I, p. 113.
Skillygoliana, No. I, p. 119.

No. IV. January, 1838.
Scenes from an Unpublished Drama (verse), p. 143.
Skillygoliana, No. II (verse), p. 157.
Chapters from the Life of Philomelus Prig, p. 169.
Skillygoliana, No. III (verse), p. 196.

No. VI. March.

The Idler, No. II, p. 223.

No. VII. April.

Skillygoliana, No. IV (partly verse), p. 274.

No. VIII. May.

A Dead Letter (verse), p. 317.

No. IX. June.

Extracts from a "Hasty Pudding Poem," p. 343.

Translations from Uhland (verse), p. 352.

CLASS POEM

CLASS POEM.

> "Some said, John, print it; others said, Not so:
> Some said, It might be good; others said, No."
>
> BUNYAN.

MDCCCXXXVIII

[Reverse] Cambridge Press: *Metcalf, Torry and Ballou.*
8vo, pp. 52, paper. Privately printed.

[iii] Dedication. To the Class of 1838, Some of whom he loves, none of whom he hates, This "Poem" is Dedicated by Their Classmate.

[v] Preface.

Many of my readers, and all my friends, know that it was not by any desire of mine that this rather slim production is printed. Circumstances known to all my readers, and which I need not dilate on here, considerably cooled my interest in the performance. Many of the lines, though in fact they would even then be indifferent good, I should prefer if possible to see in prose. *Sed Dis aliter.* Many were written merely as rough draughts, which I intended to have altered and revised, but the change of feeling, mentioned above, has prevented, and rough draughts they are still. There are a few grains of gold, at least tinsel, in the composition, but the lead — oh word infaust to poets! — will, I fear, far outweigh them. A few passages I have omitted, whose place is sufficiently well supplied by asterisks.

Paltry, however, as it is, I submit it (at their desire) to my readers, confident

> "That never anything can be amiss,
>   When simpleness and duty tender it."

Concord, Mass., August, 1838.

[7]–45, Class Poem. 47–52, Notes.

AUCTION SALE PRICES.
French and Chubbuck, February, 1904, $26.
Libbie, March, 1904, $21.
Anderson, December, 1904, $36.
Knapp, February, 1905, $82.
Alger, May, 1905, $16.
Pyser, Boston, 1906, $30.

A YEAR'S LIFE

A YEAR'S LIFE. By James Russell Lowell. Jch habe gelebt und geliebet. Boston: *C. C. Little and J. Brown.* MDCCCXLI.

16mo, pp. viii, 182. Light brown boards, paper label. Slip of errata inserted opposite p. 182. Published January, 1841.

[v] [Dedication.]

> The gentle Una I have loved,
>   The snowy maiden, pure and mild,
> Since ever by her side I roved,
>   Through ventures strange, a wandering child,
> In fantasy a Red Cross Knight,
> Burning for her dear sake to fight.
>
> If there be one who can, like her,
>   Make sunshine in life's shady places,
> One in whose holy bosom stir
>   As many gentle household graces, —
> And such I think there needs must be, —
> Will she accept this book from me?

[vii] Contents.
[1] Half-title.
[2] [Poetical Preface.]

> Hope first the gentle Poet leads,
> And he is glad to follow her;
> Kind is she, and to all his needs
> With a free hand doth minister.
>
> But, when Hope at last hath fled,
> Cometh her sister Memory;
> She wreathes Hope's garlands round her head,
> And strives to seem as fair as she.
>
> Then Hope comes back, and by the hand
> She leads a child most fair to see,
> Who with a joyous face doth stand
> Uniting Hope and Memory.
>
> So brighter grew the Earth around,
> And bluer grew the sky above;
> The Poet now his guide hath found,
> And follows in the steps of Love.

CONTENTS

To a Voice heard in Mount Auburn
On reading Spenser again
Light of mine eyes
Silent as one who treads
A gentleness that grows of steady faith
When the glad soul is full
To the Evening-star
Reading
To ——, after a Snow-storm
Sonnets on Names
   Edith
   Rose
   Mary
   Caroline
   Anne
Goe, Little Booke

NOTICES AND CRITICISMS.

C. S. Wheeler, Christian Examiner, March, 1841, v. 30, p. 131.

George S. Hiliard, North American Review, April, 1841, v. 52, p. 452.

Boston Quarterly Review, April, 1841, v. 14, p. 259.

Southern Literary Messenger, May and June, 1841, v. 7, p. 383.

Graham's Magazine, April, 1842, v. 20, p. 195.

AUCTION SALE PRICES.

Roos, Boston, 1897, $41.
Bierstadt, New York, $45.
Denny, Boston, 1906, $35.
Pyser, Boston, 1906, $45.

THE PIONEER

THE PIONEER. A Literary and Critical Magazine. J. R. Lowell and R. Carter, Editors and Proprietors. Boston: *Leland and Whiting.*

Published in January, February, and March, 1843. Lowell's contributions were as follows:

POEMS. By James Russell Lowell. Cambridge: Published by *John Owen*. MDCCCXLIV. [1843.] 16mo, pp. xii, 279, boards, paper label.

[v–vii]   To WILLIAM PAGE

MY DEAR FRIEND, —

The love between us, which can now look back upon happy years of still enduring confidence, and forward, with a sure trust in its own prophecy of yet deeper and tenderer sympathies, as long as life shall remain to us, stands in no need, I am well aware, of so poor a voucher as an Epistle Dedicatory. True, it is one of Love's chiefest charms, that it must still take special pains to be superfluous in seeking out ways to declare itself, — but for these it demands no publicity, and wishes no acknowledgement. But the admiration which one soul feels for another loses half its warmth, if it let slip any opportunity of making itself heard and felt by that strange Abbot of Unreason which we call the World. For the humblest man's true admiration is no uncertain oracle of the verdict of Posterity, — the unerring tribunal where Genius is at last allowed the right of trial by its peers, and to which none but sincere and real Greatness can appeal with an unwavering heart. There the false witnesses of to-day will be unable to appear, being fled to some hospitable Texas in the realms of Limbo, beyond the reach of its jurisdiction and the summons of its apparitors.

I have never seen the works of the Great Masters of your

Art, but I have studied their lives, and I am sure that no nobler, gentler, or purer spirit than yours was ever anointed by the Eternal Beauty to bear that part of her divine message which it belongs to the Great Painter to reveal. The sympathy of sister pursuits, of an agreeing artistic faith, and, yet more, of a common hope for the final destiny of man, has not been wanting to us, and now you will forgive the pride in having this advantage over you, namely, of telling that admiration in public which I have never stinted to utter in private. You will believe, that, as your winning that fadeless laurel, which you deserve, and which will one day surely be yours, can never heighten my judgement of you, so nothing that is not in your own control will ever lower it, and that I shall think as simply of you when the World's opinion has overtaken my own, as now.

As the swiftly diverging channels of Life bear wider and wider apart from us the friends who hoisted sail with us as fellow-mariners, when we cast off for the voyage, and as some, even, who are yet side by side with us, no longer send back to us an answering cheer, we are drawn the more closely to those that remain, and I would fain hope that this joining of our names will always be one of our not least happy memories.

And so, with all best wishes,

I remain always your friend,

J. R. LOWELL.

Cambridge, December 15, 1843.

CONTENTS

THE SAME: London *C. E. Mudie*, 1844. 12mo, p. 279, cloth.

[iv] ADVERTISEMENT TO THE ENGLISH EDITION

James Russell Lowell is a Young American Poet of great promise, whose writings have already obtained considerable reputation in his own country. The present Volume, recently published in New York, is now reprinted in London, in the belief that its thoughtfulness and beauty will commend it to the attention of the English Public; more especially as it appears to furnish a fair specimen of that new development of intellect and feeling, which renders much of the recent literature of America attractive to the minds of many Europeans.

THE SAME. London: *Routledge*. 1844.
18mo, 12mo, and post 8vo editions.

THE SAME. London: *J. Chapman*, 1844.
Post 8vo.

NOTICES AND CRITICISMS.
Democratic Review, February, 1844, v. 14, p. 215.
W. A. Davis, Christian Examiner, March, 1844, v. 36, p. 173.
Edgar Allan Poe, Graham's Magazine, March, 1844, v. 24,
p. 142. Reprinted in Harrison's edition of Poe, v. 11, p. 243.
C. C. Felton, North American Review, April, 1844, v. 58,
p. 283. Littell's Living Age, November 16, 1844, v. 3,
p. 161.
Francis Bowen, North American Review, April, 1847, v. 64,
p. 460.

AUCTION SALE PRICES.
Arnold, January, 1901, $60.
Bangs, February 13, 1901, $35.
Brown, April, 1901, $150.
McKee, May, 1902, $32.50.
Conely, October, 1902, $35.
French and Chubbuck, February 23, 1904, $4.50.

CONVERSATIONS ON SOME OF THE OLD
POETS

CONVERSATIONS ON SOME OF THE OLD POETS.
By James Russell Lowell.

"Or, if I would delight my private hours
With music or with poem, where, so soon
As in our native language, can I find
That solace."

Paradise Regained.

Cambridge : Published by *John Owen.*
MDCCCXLV. [1844.]
12mo, pp. viii, 263, cloth.

[iii] To my Father, Charles Lowell, D. D., whom, if I had not the higher privilege of revering as a parent, I should still have honored as a man and loved as a friend, this volume, containing many opinions from which he will wholly, yet with the large charity of a Christian heart, dissent, is inscribed, by his youngest child.

[iv]   "Hail, bards of mighty grasp! on you
             I chiefly call, the chosen few,
             Who cast not off the acknowledged guide,
             Who faltered not, nor turned aside,
             Whose lofty genius could survive
             Privation, under sorrow thrive."

                                        WORDSWORTH.

[v–viii]   To the Reader

A preface is always either an apology or an explanation; and a good book needs neither. That I write one, then, proves that I am diffident of the merit of this volume, to a greater degree, even, than an author must necessarily be.

For the minor faults of the book, the hurry with which it has been prepared must plead in extenuation, since it was in process of writing and printing at the same time, so that I could never estimate its proportions as a whole. This must excuse the too great length of the First Conversation, which I should have divided, had I known in time how it would have grown under my hands, which I trust the candid reader will refer to the same exculpatory cause.

The substance of two other Conversations appeared more than two years ago in the "Boston Miscellany," a magazine conducted by my friend, N. Hale, Jr., Esq. The articles, as then written, met with some approbation, and I had often been urged to reprint them by friends with whose wishes it was as well my duty as my delight to comply. Yet I felt strongly reluctant in this matter; and my reluctance increased after looking over the articles and seeing how imperfect they were.

It then occurred to me, that, by throwing them into the form of conversations, greater freedom would be given them, and that discursiveness, which was their chief fault, (among many others, of style,) would find readier pardon. Some of the deepest, as well as the most delightful books, have been written in this form in our own language, not to speak of its prevalent use among the Greeks and Latins. I need only mention the names of Isaak Walton, Walter Savage Landor, and Horne Tooke, to recall to mind three of the most prominent among many English examples.[1]

I had no intention of giving them anything like a dramatic turn, and I trust I shall not so be censured. They are merely essays, divided in this way to allow them greater ease and frankness, and the privilege of wandering at will. That this license has not been carried to a greater degree than is warranted by the usual suggestiveness of conversation will, I think, be conceded. If some of the topics introduced seem foreign to the subject, I can only say, that they are not so to my mind, and that an author's object in writing criticisms is not only to bring to light the beauties of the works he is considering, but also to express his own opinions upon those and other matters.

Wishing, as I did, to preserve, as far as possible, unaltered, whatever had given pleasure to others in the articles as already written, I experienced many difficulties. It is impossible to weld cast-iron, and I had not time to melt and recast it.

I am not bold enough to esteem these essays of any great price. Standing as yet only in the outer porch of life, I cannot be expected to report of those higher mysteries which lie unrevealed in the body of the temple. Yet, as a child, when he has found out a mean pebble, which differs from ordinary only so much as by a stripe of quartz or a stain of iron, calls his companions to behold his treasure, which to them also affords matter of delight and wonder; so I cannot but hope that my little findings may be pleasant and haply instructive to some few.

An author's opinions should be submitted to no arbitration but that of solitude and his own conscience; but many defects and blemishes in his mode of expressing them may doubtless be saved him by submitting his work, before publication, to the judgement of some loving friend — and if to the more refined eye of a woman, the better. But the haste with which these pages have been prepared and printed has precluded all but a

[1] Among the pleasantest recent writings in this form, I would mention "The Philosophy of Mystery," by W. C. Dendy, M.D.

very trifling portion of them from being judged by any eye save
my own.

Elmwood, Cambridge, Mass.,
Dec. 19, 1844.

Erratum.

Page 127, 10th line from bottom, for "superadds to the
sea keener," read "superadds to these a keener."

[Contents, as shown in the headlines.
Chaucer, 1–121
The Old Dramatists, 122–141
Chapman, 143–211
The Old Dramatists, 212–231
Ford, 233–263]

The Same.

Second edition, Cambridge: *Owen*, 1846. Same
as first.

The Same.

London edition: *Henry G. Clarke & Co.*, 1845.
Small 8vo, pp. x, 273.

The Same.

Third edition: enlarged [so-called], with introduction by Robert Ellis Thompson, Philadelphia: *David McKay*, 1893.

This edition also contains "Thomas Middleton" and
"Song-Writing," from "The Pioneer."

The Same.

In Handy Volume Classics, New York: *Crowell*,
1901.

Notices and Criticisms.

Charles Timothy Brooks, Christian Examiner, March,
1845, v. 38, p. 211.
Knickerbocker Magazine, February, 1845, v. 25, p. 166.

AUCTION SALE PRICES. First Edition.
Roos sale, March, 1900, $27.
Bangs, November 12, 1900, $20.
Arnold, January, 1901, presentation copy, $52.50.
Appleton, 1903, $40.
Bartlett, May, 1903, $100.
French and Chubbuck, February 23, 1904, $3.25.

POEMS, SECOND SERIES

POEMS. By James Russell Lowell. Second Series, Cambridge: Published by *George Nichols.* Boston: *B. B. Mussey & Co.*, 1848, [1847.] 12mo, pp. [x], 184, cloth.

[v] To the ever fresh and happy memory of our little Blanche this volume is reverently dedicated.

[vi]   To M. W. L.
         I thought our love at full, but I did err.

                    [Earlier Poems, Sonnet XXVII]

CONTENTS
Columbus
An Incident of the Fire at Hamburg
The Epitaph
Hunger and Cold
The Landlord
To a Pine-Tree
Si descendero in Infernum, ades
To the Past
To the Future
Hebe
The Search
The Present Crisis
Summer Storm
The Growth of the Legend
A Contrast
Extreme Unction
The Oak

The Royal Pedigree
Above and Below
The Captive
The Birch-Tree
An Interview with Miles Standish
On the Capture of Certain Fugitive Slaves near Washington
On the Death of Charles T. Torrey
Remembered Music
Song: to M. L.
To the Dandelion
The Ghost-Seer
The Morning-Glory [Mrs. Lowell]
Studies for Two Heads
On a Portrait of Dante by Giotto
On the Death of a Friend's Child
Anti-Texas
The Falconer
The Changeling
An Indian-Summer Reverie
The Pioneer
Longing

viii *⁎*The poem called "The Morning-Glory" on page 131,
it is proper to state, is by another hand [Mrs. Maria White
Lowell].

THE SAME. London: *Wiley*, 1848. 12mo.

NOTICES AND CRITICISMS.

W. H. Hurlbut, Christian Examiner, March, 1848, v. 44,
p. 309.

Francis Bowen, North American Review, April, 1848,
v. 66, p. 458.

AUCTION SALE PRICES.

Arnold, January, 1901, $15.
Bangs, February, 1901, $17.
Olcott, April, 1901, $10.25.
Anderson, October, 1901, $10.50.
Conely, October, 1902, $8.

French and Chubbuck, February, 1904, $6.
Knapp, February, 1905, $6.
Anderson, March, 1905, $5.50.
Anderson, April, 1905, $9.50.

A FABLE FOR CRITICS

Reader! Walk up at once (it will soon be too late) and buy at a perfectly ruinous rate a FABLE FOR CRITICS; or Better — I like, as a thing that the reader's first fancy may strike, an old-fashioned title-page, such as presents a tabular view of the volume's contents — A GLANCE AT A FEW OF OUR LITER–ARY PROGENIES (Mrs. Malaprop's word) from the Tub of Diogenes. That is, a Series of Jokes. BY A WONDERFUL QUIZ, who accompanies himself with a rub-a-dub-dub, full of spirit and grace, on the top of the tub. SET FORTH IN October the 21st day, in the year '48. By G. P. PUTNAM, Broadway.

12mo, pp. [i]–iii, [5]–78, brown cloth. Half-title, with full-page advertisement of Putnam's books on reverse, opposite title-page. Rubricated title-page, in black and red, with "That is, a Series of Jokes," in red, while "set forth in" is in black. The line, "A vocal and musical medley," is wanting. "By," before G. P. Putnam, forms a single line. Rhymed preface, in prose form (contained in all subsequent editions), occupies pp. [i]–iii. Headlines over text, with a small vignette of harp on last page. Cloth of the binding is a dark-brown muslin, with simple brown stamp on sides, with publisher's monogram in a shield in the middle, and plain gold lettering on the back.

In this edition there are several misprints. Page 25, line 10, has "cotilion;" and page 40, line 21, "Goliah." In a letter to Sydney Howard Gay, December 20, 1848, Lowell writes, "Briggs must give you a copy of the second edition, in which the atrocious misprints of the other will be corrected."

The first edition was advertised for October 20, and was ready for the public on the 25th. The title-page stated the date of its publication as the 21st, which was in later editions changed to the 31st. The first edition was of 1000 copies, was printed from type, and the forms were distributed as soon as the printing was completed. This may in part account for the numerous misprints.

In Putnam's Book-list for 1848 appeared this announcement:

Fable for Critics: A New Satirical Poem; or, A Glance at a Few of Our Literary Progenies. By a Wonderful Quiz. 1 Vol., 12mo, boards, 50 cents; cloth, 63 cents.

*₌*The "Fable" is full of a genial humor, and abounds in most felicitous satire at our men and women of letters, some of whom are sketched with inimitable skill and truthfulness.

THE SAME. Second Edition.

Reader! Walk up at once (it will soon be too late) and buy at a perfectly ruinous rate a FABLE FOR CRITICS; or, Better (I like, as a thing that the reader's first fancy may strike, an old-fashioned title-page, such as presents a tabular view of the volume's contents) A GLANCE AT A FEW OF OUR LITERARY PROGENIES (Mrs. Malaprop's word) from the Tub of Diogenes; A

Vocal and Musical Medley. That is, a Series of Jokes. BY A WONDERFUL QUIZ, who accompanies himself with a rub-a-dub-dub, full of spirit and grace, on the top of the tub. SET FORTH IN October, the 21st day, in the year '48. G. P. PUTNAM, Broadway.

The title-page of the second edition differs in several essential respects from the first. "A vocal and musical medley" has been added, and "by" before the publisher's name has been omitted. The parenthetical clause, "I like, . . . contents," has been enclosed in parentheses. In some copies of this edition the publisher's address is changed, as noted hereafter.

The second edition was stereotyped and appeared early in January, 1849. Some of the misprints were corrected; but a curious one remained on page 54, line 18, where "censor" appears in place of "censer," thus spoiling both the meaning and the pun. Three printings of this edition seem to have taken place in 1849 (though each has been called an edition); the first in January, the second in February, and the third in November. It is very difficult to distinguish the several printings of the second edition, five or six copies with distinctive features having been examined, two of which appear to have been printed or bound-up in November. In one of these the rhymed preface occupies pp. [iii]–v; text, pp. [7]–80. There are no headlines, and the vignette on last page is absent. The only signature is 2* on page 33. No advertisements. In another copy there is no half-title; and the names of the printers, Leavitt, Trow & Co., appear on reverse of title-page. "A Preliminary Note to the Second Edition" follows the title-leaf, unpaged, and is succeeded by the rhymed preface, paged [iii]–v. Putnam's advertisement at the end is dated November, 1848. The matter on each page is identical with the first

edition, but the type is different, and the pagination is
two pages ahead in all printings of the second; that is,
page 7 of the second corresponds to page 5 of the first
edition. There is no ruled headline. In another copy
the rhymed preface is first and is followed by the preliminary note.

What appears to be a fourth printing gives the address
of Putnam as 10 Park Place, date same as in first edition,
with rhyme left imperfect. In 1890 Lowell wrote: " Mr.
Putnam, I believe, never discovered that the title-page
was in metre, nor that it was in rhyme either. Mr. Norton told me the other day that he had a copy of some
later edition (after Putnam had changed his place of
business), in which the imprint was ' G. P. Putnam,
Astor (or something) Place.' I don't remember whether
I knew of it at the time, but had I known, I should have
let it pass as adding to the humor of the book." This
edition has no advertising pages, and the " Preliminary
Note" is after the rhymed preface. Muslin binding,
blind stamp on sides, with oval in centre, and blind lines
at the top and bottom of the back.

THE SAME. Fifth edition, Boston: *Ticknor and
Fields*, 1856.

12mo. Bottom of title-page after "top of the
tub" omitted. Matter on each page the same,
but different type. "Candid remarks to the
Reader," pp. [iii]–v. "Preliminary Note," pp.
[1]–6. Text, pp. [7]–80. *Ticknor and Fields'*
"New Books and New Editions " occupy 12
pages at end, dated March, 1856.

POETICAL WORKS, Boston: *Ticknor & Fields*,
1857.

Two vols.

The second volume opens with "A Fable for Critics." In all previous editions the headline had been, "A Fable for *the* Critics," but in this one it is made to conform to the title-page. ¡ In the first and subsequent editions the date had been "October the 21st day," but in this one it is changed for the first time to "October the 31st day," which has been since retained.

A FABLE FOR CRITICS, by James Russell Lowell. With vignette Portraits of the Authors de˙quibus fabula narratur. [Riverside Press] vignette. Boston and New York: *Houghton, Mifflin and Company*, MDCCCXCI. [October, 1890.] 12mo, pp. 101, cloth.

Opposite title-page the rubricated title-page as in second edition. *Putnam.* '48.

[4] To Charles F. Briggs this volume is affectionately inscribed.
[5] This *jeu d'esprit* was extemporized, I may fairly say, so rapidly was it written, purely for my own amusement and with no thought of publication. I sent daily instalments of it to a friend in New York, the late Charles F. Briggs. He urged me to let it be printed, and I at last consented to its anonymous publication. The secret was kept till several persons had laid claim to its authorship.

THE SAME.
Riverside Literature Series, no. M.

NOTICES AND CRITICISMS.
Democratic Review, December, 1848, v. 23, p. 564.
Francis Bowen, North American Review, January, 1849, v. 68, p. 192.
Thomas Hughes, Critic, v. 8, p. 152.
Edgar Allan Poe, in "On Poetry and the Poets," Griswold's edition of Poe, v. 3, p. 275; Woodberry's edition, v. 6, p. 240.
Littell's Living Age, March 16, 1849, v. 92, p. 681.

AUCTION SALE PRICES. First Edition.
  Roos, March, 1900, $7.50.
  Bangs, May, 1900, $13.
  McKee, November, 1900, $18.
  Bangs, January, 1902, $20.
  Appleton, April, 1903, $11.50.
  Anderson, January, 1904, $11.50.
  French and Chubbuck, February, 1904, $8.
  Anderson, April, 1905, $21.
  Gordon, April, 1905, $17.

THE BIGLOW PAPERS, FIRST SERIES

Melibœus-Hipponax. THE BIGLOW PAPERS, Edited, with an Introduction, Notes, Glossary, and Copious Index, by Homer Wilbur, A. M., Pastor of the First Church of Jalaam, and (Prospective) member of many Literary, Learned and Scientific societies (*for which see page v*).

> The ploughman's whistle, or the trivial flute,
> Finds more respect than great Apollo's lute.
> > *Quarles Emblems*, B. ii, E. 8.

Margaritas, munde porcine, calcasti: en, siliquas accipe.
> *Jac. Car. Fil. ad Pub. Leg.* 1.

Cambridge: Published by *George Nichols*. New York: *George P. Putnam*, 155 Broadway, 1848.

12mo, pp. xxxii, 163, cloth.

Pp. 1–12, preceding title, contained "Notices of an Independent Press;" [v]–vii, Note to title-page; viii, titles of Wilbur; [ix]–xxi, Introduction. The poems entitled "The Two Gunners" and "Leaving the Matter open" were added in later editions.

Part of this edition was printed with, and part with-

out, the "Notices of an Independent Press," preceding
title.

CONTENTS.

THE CHOICEST HUMOROUS POETRY OF THE AGE.

THE BIGLOW PAPERS.   Alluded to by John Bright
in the House of Commons, with additional
Notes, an enlarged Glossary, and an Illustration
by George Cruikshank.   London: *John Camden
Hotten*, 1859.

16mo, pp. xvi, 198, brown cloth.

With "Preface to the present Edition by John Camden Hotten," dated "Piccadilly, Oct. 25, 1859." This was a "pirated" edition.

THE SAME. Fourth edition. Boston: *Ticknor and Fields*, 1857. Pp. xxxii, 163.

THE SAME. Newly edited, with a Preface by the Author of "Tom Brown's School-days." Reprinted, with the Author's sanction, from the fourth American edition. London: *Trübner & Co.*, 1859.

12mo, pp. xli, 140.

Thomas Hughes's preface occupies twenty pages.

NOTICES AND CRITICISMS.
Literary World, December 2, 1848, v. 3, p. 872.
Francis Bowen, North American Review, January, 1849, v. 68, p. 183.
D. March, New Englander, February, 1849, v. 7, p. 63.
Littell's Living Age, "Yankee Humor," March 16, 1849, v. 92, p. 681.

AUCTION SALE PRICES. First Edition.
Arnold, January, 1901, $21.
Roos, March, 1900, $10.
Bangs, May, 1900, $13.
Libbey, May, 1901, $12.62.
Morgan, April, 1902, $10.
Bangs, November, 1902, $7.75.
Bangs, April, 1899, $16.
Anderson, January, 1905, $12.
Denny, January, 1906, $10.
Pyser, February, 1906, $18.

THE VISION OF SIR LAUNFAL

THE VISION OF SIR LAUNFAL. By James Russell Lowell. Cambridge: Published by *George Nichols*, 1848.

16mo, pp. 27, cloth.

Introductory matter not paged, but the "Note," which has appeared in all editions, was printed on page succeeding title-leaf.

A second edition appeared in 1849, and a third in 1850.

THE SAME. By James Russell Lowell. Fourth Edition. Boston: *Ticknor, Reed, and Fields*, MDCCCLI.

Pp. [9]–33.

Note opposite title-leaf.

THE SAME. Illustrated edition. Boston: *Ticknor & Fields*, 1866.

16mo, pp. 29, cloth. Illustrations by Sol. Eytinge, Jr.

THE VISION OF SIR LAUNFAL, THE CATHEDRAL, FAVORITE POEMS. *James R. Osgood & Co.*, 1876.

16mo, pp. 108. Illustrated.

Modern Classics, no. 5.

CONTENTS:

The Vision of Sir Launfal
The Cathedral
My Love
Above and Below
The Changeling
The Shepherd of King Admetus
Ambrose
Masaccio

An Incident of the Fire at Hamburg
To the Dandelion
Beaver Brook
An Interview with Miles Standish
The Courtin'
What Mr. Robinson thinks
Mr. Hosea Biglow to the Editor of the Atlantic Monthly
To Charles Eliot Norton
The First Snow-Fall
Without and Within
Godminster Chimes
Auf Wiedersehen
Palinode
After the Burial
The Dead House
Yussouf
What Rabbi Jehosha said
All-Saints
The Darkened Mind
An Ember Picture
To H. W. L.
The Nightingale in the Study
In the Twilight
The Foot-Path
The Washers of the Shroud

THE SAME. London: *Sampson, Low & Co.*, 1876. Same as Boston edition of 1866.

THE VISION OF SIR LAUNFAL. Louisville: *American Printing House for the Blind*, 1878.
> 4to, pp. 15.
> In raised letters for the use of the blind.

THE VISION OF SIR LAUNFAL, and Thirty-three Other Poems. Boston: *The Howe Memorial Printing House*, 1881.
> 4to, pp. 161.
> In raised letters for the use of the blind.

THE VISION OF SIR LAUNFAL, AND OTHER POEMS.
Boston: *Houghton, Mifflin & Company*, 1887.
16mo, pp. xii, 113. Biographical Sketch,
Notes, Portraits, and Other Illustrations, and
Aids to the Study of the Vision of Sir Launfal,
by H. A. Davidson.

Riverside Literature Series, no. 30.

CONTENTS

A Few References for the Study of Lowell's Life and Works
The Indebtedness of the Author of the Vision of Sir Launfal
to Other Writers
Topics for Study

THE VISION OF SIR LAUNFAL, AND OTHER POEMS.
Boston: *Houghton, Mifflin & Co.*, 1900.
16mo, pp. viii, 138. Critical and Biographical
Introductions.

Riverside Aldine Classics.

CONTENTS
Note
The Vision of Sir Launfal
A Fable for Critics
Ode Recited at the Harvard Commemoration

THE VISION OF SIR LAUNFAL. Boston: *Houghton,
Mifflin & Co.*
32mo, pp. 78. Illustrated.
Lilliput Classics.

THE VISION OF SIR LAUNFAL, AND OTHER POEMS.
Edited, with Introduction and Notes, by Ellen
A. Vinton. Boston: *Sanborn & Co.*, 1889.
16mo, pp. xxix, 63. Portrait.
Cambridge Literature Series, no. 4.

THE VISION OF SIR LAUNFAL. Boston: *Houghton,
Mifflin & Co.*, 1890. (September.)
Japanese paper edition.

THE SAME. Boston: *Houghton, Mifflin & Co.*,
1890. (October.)
Regular Holiday Edition.

THE SAME: with biography, critical opinions, and notes. New York: *Maynard, Merrill & Co.*, 1894.

16mo, Portrait.

English Classic Series, no. 129.

THE VISION OF SIR LAUNFAL. Edited, with notes, etc. Boston: *Leach, Shewell & Sanborn*, 1896. 16mo.

Students' series of English Classics.

THE VISION OF SIR LAUNFAL, AND OTHER POEMS. Introduction by H. Bates. New York: *Macmillan*, 1900.

18mo.

Pocket American Classics.

THE SAME. Notes by F. R. Lane. New York: *Allyn & Bacon*, 1900.

12mo.

THE SAME. Biography and notes, by Margaret H. McCarter. Topeka: *Crane & Co.*, 1904.

AID TO THE STUDY AND TEACHING OF THE VISION OF SIR LAUNFAL, by Graham. San Francisco: *Whitaker & Ray*.

THE VISION OF SIR LAUNFAL, AND OTHER POEMS. With biographical sketch, notes, and illustrations. Boston: *Houghton, Mifflin & Co.*, 1906.

16mo, pp. xviii, 96.

Riverside School Library.

[101]

Contents

A Sketch of the Life of James Russell Lowell
    i. Elmwood
    ii. Education
    iii. First Ventures
    iv. Verse and Prose
    v. Public Life
Introductory Note
The Vision of Sir Launfal
    Prelude to Part First
    Part First
    Prelude to Part Second
    Part Second
Ode Recited at the Harvard Commemoration
On Board the '76
An Indian-Summer Reverie
The First Snow-Fall
The Oak
Prometheus
To W. L. Garrison
Wendell Phillips
Mr. Hosea Biglow to the Editor of the Atlantic Monthly
Villa Franca
The Nightingale in the Study
Aladdin
Beaver Brook
The Shepherd of King Admetus
The Present Crisis
Al Fresco
The Foot-Path

Notices and Criticisms.

Orestes A. Brownson, Brownson's Quarterly Review, April, 1849, v. 6, p. 265. Brownson's Works, v. 19, p. 308.

R. C. Pitman, Methodist Quarterly Review, January, 1850, Fourth series, v. 2, p. 107.

Littell's Living Age, April 20, 1867, v. 93, p. 179.

Poet-Lore, January, 1894, v. 6, p. 47.

Auction Sale Prices. First Edition.

Arnold, January, 1901, $35.

Bangs, January, 1902, $19.

Presentation Copy, January, 1903, $115.
Somerby, December, 1903, $13.
Anderson, December, 1905, $40.
Denny, January, 1906, $26.
Pyser, February, 1906, $31.
Merwin-Clayton, New York, February, 1906, $29.

POEMS, 1849

POEMS. By James Russell Lowell. In two Volumes. Vol. I. Boston: *Ticknor, Reed and Fields,* MDCCCXLIX.

16mo, vol. i, pp. xii, 251; vol. ii, pp. vii, 254, boards.

[viii] This edition is a revised one, but as the volumes which form the substance of it had been stereotyped, it was found easier to cancel than to correct. Accordingly several poems and parts of poems have been left out of the first volume, and their places supplied in most instances by selections from an earlier volume, published in 1841. These intercalated pieces will be found sufficiently designated by the dates appended to each.

The second volume has been made correspondent in size with its fellows, by the addition of some poems more lately written.

CONTENTS OF VOL. I.
A Legend of Brittany
Part I
Part II
Miscellaneous Poems
Threnodia
The Sirens
Serenade
Irene
Prometheus
Song, "Violet! sweet violet!"
Rosaline
Allegra
The Fountain

CONTENTS OF VOL. II

POEMS. London: *Routledge*, 1851–52.
12mo and 18mo editions.

NOTICES AND CRITICISMS.
Literary World, January 12, 1850, v. 6, p. 35.
Brownson's Quarterly Review, April, 1850, v. 4 n. s., p. 271.

AUCTION SALE PRICES. First Edition.
Arnold, January, 1901, $12.50.
Bangs, February, 1901, $21.
Libbie, March, 1901, $21.
Peirce, May, 1903, $13.
Anderson, January, 1904, $6.20.
French and Chubbuck, February, 1904, $5.
Libbie, June, 1904, with inserted letter, $10.
Anderson, March, 1905, $6.

POEMS OF MARIA LOWELL

THE POEMS OF MARIA LOWELL. Cambridge:
Privately Printed, 1855.
Square 12mo, pp. vi, 68, cloth. "Poems by
Maria Lowell" printed in gilt on front cover;
gilt edges. Portrait opposite title-page, from
a drawing by Seth Cheney after the painting
by William Page.

Only 50 copies were printed, for distribution to Mrs.
Lowell's friends.

[iii] To Emelyn Story, Mary Lowell Putnam, and Sarah B.
Shaw, this book is dedicated.

CONTENTS
The Maiden's Harvest
Song
The Alpine Sheep
Africa
Jesus and the Dove
The Morning-Glory

The Slave-Mother
Necklaces
Cadiz
Rome
The Grave of Keats
Avignon
Rouen, Place de la Pucelle
The Sick-Room
An Opium Fantasy
Sonnet
Sonnet
Sonnet
Sonnet
Memories of Waters

NOTICES AND CRITICISMS.

Poet-Lore, January, 1898, v. 10, p. 19. "Mrs. Lowell's
'Africa.'"

Poet-Lore, v. 10, pp. 19, 22. "Mrs. Lowell's Poems,"
by Caroline Healy Dall.

AUCTION SALE PRICES.

Arnold, January, 1890, $90.
McKee, November, 1900, $87.
Bangs, April, 1901, $95.
Bartlett, May, 1903, presentation copy, $210.
Anderson, December, 1904, $35.
Knapp, February, 1905, $60.
Pyser, February, 1906, $85.

FIRESIDE TRAVELS

FIRESIDE TRAVELS. By James Russell Lowell.

" Travelling makes a man sit still in his old age with sat-
isfaction, and travel over the world again in his chair and bed
by discourse and thoughts."

The Voyage of Italy, by RICHARD LASSELS, Gent.

[Publishers' monogram.] Boston: *Ticknor and
Fields*, 1864 [August].

16mo, pp. [x], 324, cloth.

[iii]   To W. W. S[TORY].

Who carves his thoughts in marble will not scorn
These pictured bubbles, if so far they fly;
They will recall days ruddy but with morn,
Not red like those late past or drawing nigh!

[v] The greater part of this volume was printed ten years ago in
"Putnam's Monthly" and "Graham's Magazine." The additions (most of them about Italy) have been made up, as the original
was, from old letters and journals written on the spot. My wish
was to describe not so much what I went to see, as what I saw
that was most unlike what one sees at home. If the reader find
entertainment, he will find all I hoped to give him.

CONTENTS:
Cambridge Thirty Years Ago
A Moosehead Journal
Letters from my Journal in Italy and Elsewhere
At Sea
In the Mediterranean
Italy
A few Bits of Roman Mosaic

A list of Lowell's books is printed opposite the title-page.
At the end is the "List of Books published by Ticknor and
Fields," dated September, 1864, 22 pp., followed by an ad-
vertisement of the Atlantic Monthly.

THE SAME. By James Russell Lowell, Author of
"The Biglow Papers." London and Cambridge: *Macmillan & Co.*, 1864.
12mo, pp. 341.

A MOOSEHEAD JOURNAL, AT SEA. Boston: *James
R. Osgood & Co.*, 1877.
32mo, illustrated, pp. 75.
Vest Pocket Series.

FIRESIDE TRAVELS. Boston: *Houghton, Mifflin & Co.*, 1885.

Riverside Aldine Series, no. 3.

THE SAME. Boston: *Houghton, Mifflin & Co.*, 1897.

16mo, pp. 282.
Riverside Aldine Series.

THE SAME. Boston: *Houghton, Mifflin & Co.*, 1899 [September, 1898].

Crown 8vo, pp. 324, gilt top.
Cambridge Classics.

NOTICES AND CRITICISMS.
Christian Examiner, November, 1864, v. 77, p. 376.
Spectator, October 8, 1864, v. 37, p. 1157.
Athenæum, November 12, 1864, p. 629.

AUCTION SALE PRICES. First Edition.
French and Chubbuck, February, 1904, $3.50.
Knapp, February, 1905, $3.25.
Smalley, April, 1905, Charles Dickens copy of 1865 edition, $6.75.

THE PRESIDENT'S POLICY

No. 16. THE PRESIDENT'S POLICY. By James Russell Lowell. From the North American Review. [Philadelphia: Printed by *Crissy & Markley* for the Union League of Philadelphia, 1864.]

8vo, pp. 22, paper.

Two editions of this pamphlet were printed, both in Philadelphia by the Union League in its numbered series of pamphlets.

NOTICES AND CRITICISMS.

Lincoln's Complete Works, edition of Nicolay and Hay, v. 2, p. 470.

North American Review, April, 1864, v. 98, p. 630.

The Bibliographer, "A Rare Lowell Item," June, 1902, v. 1, p. 233.

Theodore Wesley Koch, "Lowell's Pamphlet, 'The President's Policy,' 1864," The Bibliographer, February, 1903, v. 2, p. 107.

AUCTION SALE PRICES.

Anderson, December, 1903, $55.

Anderson, January, 1904, $49.

Anderson, January, 1905, $41.

Knapp, February, 1905, $78.

COMMEMORATION ODE

ODE RECITED AT THE COMMEMORATION OF THE LIVING AND DEAD SOLDIERS OF HARVARD UNIVERSITY, July 21, 1865. Cambridge: Privately Printed, 1865.

8vo, boards, paper label, gilt top.

Only 50 copies printed, for Lowell's use.

AUCTION SALE PRICES.

Libbie, May, 1900, $60.

Arnold, January, 1901, presentation copy to F. H. Underwood, $220.

French, April, 1901, presentation to John Bartlett, $410.

Whipple, April, 1903, presentation copy, $400.

Pyser, January, 1906, $531.

THE BIGLOW PAPERS. SECOND SERIES

Meliboeus-Hipponax. THE BIGLOW PAPERS. Second Series. [There follow quotations from Longinus, Montaigne, Fischart, Quintilianus, and Jasmin, as given in all editions. Also monogram of the Publishers.] Boston: *James R. Osgood and Company*, late *Ticknor & Fields*, and *Fields, Osgood & Co.*, 1867. [October, 1866.]

16mo, pp. lxxx, 258, cloth.

On reverse of title-page appear quotations from Quintilianus, Cronica Jocelini, and Henri Beyle, which follow those mentioned above as appearing in all editions.

[i]   To E. R. Hoar

The introduction, pp. [v]–lxxvi, is devoted to an essay on the Yankee form of the English speech; and pp. lxxvii–lxxx contain "The Courtin'" in its completed form.

CONTENTS
    Introduction
        The Courtin'
        No. I. Birdofredum Sawin, Esq., to Mr. Hosea Biglow
        No. II. Mason and Slidell: A Yankee Idyll
        No. III. Birdofredum Sawin, Esq., to Mr. Hosea Biglow
        No. IV. A Message of Jeff Davis in Secret Session
        No. V. Speech of Honourable Preserved Doe in Secret Caucus
        No. VI. Sunthin' in the Pastoral Line
        No. VII. Latest Views of Mr. Biglow
        No. VIII. Kettelopotomachia
        No. IX. Table-Talk
        No. X. Mr. Hosea Biglow to the Editor of the Atlantic Monthly
        No. XI. Mr. Hosea Biglow's Speech in March Meeting
    Index

THE SAME, Second Series, Parts 1 to 3. London: *Trübner*, 1862.

12mo.

THE SAME. Notes and Introduction by the editor
of Artemus Ward; colored illustrations by
George Cruikshank. London: *Hotten*, 1865.
16mo, gilt top.

THE SAME. Montreal: *R. Worthington*, 1866.
8vo, pp. xii, 55, double columns.

YANKEE DROLLERIES. First and Second Series.
The most celebrated works of the best Ameri-
can humorists. With an introduction by George
Augustus Sala. London: *Routledge*, 1867.
> These volumes contain respectively the two series of
> the Biglow Papers.

THE BIGLOW PAPERS. Both Series. London:
Hotten, 1877. Introduction by George Augustus Sala.

THE SAME. Both Series. Preface by Thomas
Hughes. London: *Trübner*, 1880.
Post 8vo, cloth.

THE SAME. Boston: *Houghton, Mifflin and Co.*,
1885.
> 16mo, pp. vi, 193; viii, 199.
> Riverside Aldine Series, nos. 8 and 9; the two series
> of the Biglow Papers.

THE SAME. London: *Routledge*, 1886.
16mo, pp. 384.
"Routledge's Pocket Library."

THE RUSSELL LOWELL (HOSEA BIGLOW) BIRTH-
DAY BOOK. London: *Routledge*, 1887.
16mo, pp. 288.

THE BIGLOW PAPERS. Boston: *Houghton, Mifflin and Co.*, January, 1891.

THE SAME. Boston: *Houghton, Mifflin and Co.*,
1894.
> Crown 8vo, pp. 564; crimson cloth, gilt top.
> Cambridge Classics.

THE SAME. Boston: *Houghton, Mifflin and Co.*,
1896.
> New edition.

Humorous Books. THE BIGLOW PAPERS. Complete edition, reprinted from the original. London: *Routledge*, 1898.
> 12mo, pp. 96.

AUTOGRAPH LEAVES OF OUR COUNTRY'S
AUTHORS. Baltimore: *Cushing & Bailey*, 1864.
> 4to, pp. xi, 200, cloth.

> In this book, issued by the Sanitary Commission Fair,
edited by John P. Kennedy and Alexander Bliss, "The
Courtin'" first appeared in its completed form, as after-
wards published in the second series. "The Courtin'"
is on pp. 107–112.

THE COURTIN'. Boston: *James R. Osgood and
Co.*, 1874. [December 1, 1873.] Illustrated in
silhouette by Winslow Homer.
> 4to, plates.

> NOTICES AND CRITICISMS.
>> Spectator, "The New Biglow Papers," October 1, 1864,
v. 37, p. 1133.
>> J. R. Dennett, The Nation, November 15, 1866, v. 3, p. 386.

Littell's Living Age, "Yankee Humor," March 16, 1866,
v. 92, p. 681.
William Dean Howells, Atlantic Monthly, January, 1867,
v. 19, p. 123.
British Quarterly Review, "American Humor," October,
1870, v. 52, p. 324.
Atlantic Monthly, "The Courtin'," February, 1874, v. 33,
p. 235.
Cornhill, "Mr. Lowell's Poems," January, 1875, v. 31, p. 65.
Hugh Reginald Haweis, American Humorists, 1882.
Joseph Henry Gilmore, Chautauquan, April, 1896, v. 23,
p. 19.

AUCTION SALE PRICES. First Edition.
Arnold, January, 1901, John Fiske's copy, $11.
French, April, 1901, presentation copy, $70.
Peirce, May, 1903, presentation copy, $60.
Libbie, June, 1904, $31.
Merwin-Clayton, March 3, 1905, $5.50.
Gordon, April, 1905, $3.

UNDER THE WILLOWS

UNDER THE WILLOWS AND OTHER POEMS. By
James Russell Lowell. Boston: *Fields, Osgood & Co.*, successors to *Ticknor and Fields,*
1869. [November, 1868.]

12mo, pp. [vi], 286, cloth, vignette of willow
in gilt on front cover; same as blind stamp on
back cover.

"Erratum" slip opposite page 286.

[iii]-v. To Charles Eliot Norton, Agro Dolce.
[vi] [*₊* No collection of the author's poems has been made since
1848, and some of those in this volume date back even farther
than that. All but two of the shortest have been printed before,
either wholly or in part. As the greater number, however, were

published more than fifteen years ago, they will have, perhaps, something of novelty to most readers. A few pieces, more strictly comic, have been omitted, as out of keeping; and "Fitz Adam's Story," which some good friends will miss, is also left to stand over, because it belongs to a connected series, which, it is hoped, may be completed if the days should be propitious.]

CONTENTS

A Winter-Evening Hymn to my Fire
Fancy's Casuistry
To Mr. John Bartlett
Ode to Happiness
Villa Franca
The Miner
Gold Egg: A Dream-Fantasy
A Familiar Epistle to a Friend
An Ember Picture
To H. W. L.
The Nightingale in the Study
In the Twilight
The Foot-Path
Poems of the War
  The Washers of the Shroud
  Two Scenes from the Life of Blondel
  Memoriæ Positum
  On Board the '76
  Ode Recited at the Harvard Commemoration
L'Envoi — To the Muse

NOTICES AND CRITICISMS.

William Dean Howells, Atlantic Monthly, February, 1869,
  v. 23, p. 262.
Spectator, "Mr. Lowell's Poems," February 6, 1869, v. 42,
  p. 168.
Athenæum, April 17, 1869, p. 531.

AUCTION SALE PRICES.

French, April, 1901, $20. Another, presentation copy, $26.
Whipple, April, 1903, presentation copy, $27.50.
French and Chubbuck, February, 1904, $3.50.

THE CATHEDRAL

THE CATHEDRAL. By James Russell Lowell.
[Publishers' monogram.] Boston: *Fields, Osgood & Co.*, 1870. [December, 1869.]

  16mo, pp. 53, cloth.

The Cathedral was published in the Atlantic Monthly, January, 1870, v. 25, p. 1; and it was included in the Poetical Works of 1877.

THE CATHEDRAL and the HARVARD COMMEMO-RATION ODE. Boston: *James R. Osgood & Co.*, 1877.

32mo, pp. 96, cloth. Illustrations.

Vest Pocket Series.

NOTICES AND CRITICISMS.

William Cleaver Wilkinson, Baptist Quarterly, v. 4, p. 374; Hours at Home, v. 10, p. 541.

J. R. Dennett, Nation, January 27, 1870, v. 10, p. 60.

AUCTION SALE PRICES. First edition.

Whipple, April, 1903, presentation copy, $47.50.

Anderson, March, 1904, $10.

AMONG MY BOOKS

AMONG MY BOOKS. By James Russell Lowell, A. M., Professor of Belles-Lettres in Harvard College. Boston: *Fields, Osgood & Co.*, 1870. [February.]

12mo, pp. [vi], 380, cloth.

[iii] To F. L. D.

Love comes and goes with music in his feet,
And tunes young pulses to his roundelays:
Love brings thee this: will it persuade thee, Sweet,
That he turns proser when he comes and stays?

CONTENTS

Dryden
Witchcraft
Shakespeare Once More
New England Two Centuries Ago
Lessing
Rousseau and the Sentimentalists

[118]

THE SAME. Six Essays. By J. Russell Lowell.
London: *Macmillan*, 1870.

NOTICES AND CRITICISMS.

Athenæum, March 19, 1870, p. 379.
George W. W. Durgee, Nation, April 21, 1870, v. 10, p. 258.
William Dean Howells, Atlantic Monthly, June, 1870, v. 25,
p. 757.
Academy, July 9, 1870, v. 1, p. 252.

AUCTION SALE PRICES. First edition.

Bangs, March, 1901, $5.66.
Appleton, April, 1903, $11.
French and Chubbuck, February, 1904, $3.75.
Anderson, March, 1904, $4.50.
Libbie, June, 1904, $12.12.

MY STUDY WINDOWS

MY STUDY WINDOWS. By James Russell Lowell,
A. M., Professor of Belles-Lettres in Harvard
College. [Publishers' monogram.] Boston:
James R. Osgood & Co., late *Ticknor and
Fields*, and *Fields, Osgood & Co.*, 1871. [January 20.]

12mo, pp. [vi], 433, cloth.

[iii] PREFATORY NOTE.

My former volume of Essays has been so kindly received that
I am emboldened to make another and more miscellaneous collection. The papers here gathered have been written at intervals
during the last fifteen years, and I knew no way so effectual to
rid my mind of them and make ready for a new departure, as
this of shutting them between two covers where they can haunt
me, at least, no more. I should have preferred a simpler title,
but publishers nowadays are inexorable on this point, and I was
too much occupied for happiness of choice. That which I have
desperately snatched is meant to imply both the books within
and the world without, and perhaps may pass muster in the case
of one who has always found his most fruitful study in the
open air.

[119]

[iv] To Professor F. J. Child

My dear Child, —

You were good enough to like my Essay on Chaucer (about whom you know so much more than I), and I shall accordingly so far presume upon our long friendship as to inscribe the volume containing it with your name.

Always heartily yours,

J. R. Lowell.

Cambridge, Christmas, 1870.

Contents

My Garden Acquaintance
A Good Word for Winter
On a Certain Condescension in Foreigners
A Great Public Character
Carlyle
Abraham Lincoln
The Life and Letters of James Gates Percival
Thoreau
Swinburne's Tragedies
Chaucer
Library of Old Authors
Emerson, the Lecturer
Pope

The Same. London: *Sampson, Low & Co.*, 1871.

16mo.

In "Low's Copyright Series of American Authors."

The Same. 1874.

8vo.

In Rose Library.

The Same. With an Introduction by Richard Garnett, LL. D. London: *Walter Scott*, 1887.

16mo, pp. xvi, 378.

In Camelot series; also in Shilling series.

Notices and Criticisms.

Athenæum, April 22, 1871, p. 490.

Spectator, May 13, 1871, v. 44, p. 579.

William Dean Howells, Atlantic Monthly, June, 1871, v. 27, p. 778.

AUCTION SALE PRICES.   First Edition.

Bangs, May, 1900, $10.

French, April, 1901, presentation copy, $45.

Whipple, April, 1903, presentation copy, $30.

French and Chubbuck, February, 1904, $3.50.

AMONG MY BOOKS

AMONG MY BOOKS. Second Series. By James Russell Lowell, Professor of Belles-Lettres in Harvard College. [Publishers' monogram.] Boston: *James R. Osgood & Co.*, late *Ticknor & Fields*, and *Fields, Osgood & Co.*, 1876. [December, 1875.]

12mo, pp. [vi], 327, cloth.

[iii]   TO R. W. EMERSON

A love and honor which more than thirty years have deepened, though priceless to him they enrich, are of little import to one capable of inspiring them. Yet I cannot deny myself the pleasure of so far intruding on your reserve as at least to make public my acknowledgment of the debt I can never repay.

CONTENTS

Dante

Spenser

Wordsworth

Milton

Keats.

THE SAME.   Second Series.   London: *Sampson, Snow & Co.*, 1876.

Post 8vo.

NOTICES AND CRITICISMS.

Scribner's Magazine, v. 11, p. 747.

Century, Culture and Progress, v. 11, p. 747.
Edward Dowden, Academy, March 11, 1876, v. 9, p. 232.
William Dean Howells, Atlantic Monthly, April, 1876, v. 37, p. 493.
Spectator, July 22, 1876, v. 49, p. 925.

AUCTION SALE PRICES.   First Edition.

Arnold, January, 1901, $16.
French and Chubbuck, February, 1904, $8.
Libbie, March, 1904, $3.25.
Anderson, March, 1905, $3.62.
Pyser, February, 1906, $23. Same copy as above.

THREE MEMORIAL POEMS

THREE MEMORIAL POEMS.   By James Russell LOWELL. Εἶς οἰωνὸς ἄριστος ἀμύνεσαι περὶ πάτρης. Boston: *James R. Osgood & Co.*, late *Ticknor & Fields*, and *Fields, Osgood & Co.*, 1877. [December, 1876.]

16mo, pp. [13]–92, cloth.

[8] Sonnet of dedication.

CONTENTS
  Ode Read at Concord, April 19, 1875
  Under the Old Elm
  An Ode for the Fourth of July, 1876

NOTICES AND CRITICISMS.
  William Dean Howells, Atlantic Monthly, March, 1877, v. 39, p. 374.
  James Vila Blake, Radical Review, May, 1877, v. 1, p. 174.

AUCTION SALE PRICES.
  Arnold, January, 1901, letter inserted, $6.50.

THE ROSE

THE ROSE. By James Russell Lowell. With
Illustrations. [Publishers' vignette.] Boston:
James R. Osgood & Co., 1878.

Square 12mo, not paged ; cloth.

First separate edition.

ON DEMOCRACY

Birmingham and Midland Institute. ON DE-
MOCRACY: An Address delivered in the Town
Hall, Birmingham, on the 6th of October,
1884. By His Excellency, The Hon. James
Russell Lowell, D. C. L., LL. D., American
Minister in London, President. Birmingham:
Printed by *Coud Bros.*, Paternoster Row,
Moor Street, 1884.

DEMOCRACY AND OTHER ADDRESSES. By James
Russell Lowell. [Publishers' vignette.] Boston
and New York: *Houghton, Mifflin & Co.*, The
Riverside Press, Cambridge, 1887. [November,
1886.]

16mo, pp. vi, 245, cloth.

[iii] To G. W. SMALLEY, Esq.

MY DEAR SMALLEY, — You heard several of these Addresses
delivered, and were good enough to think better of them than
I did. As this was one of my encouragements to repeat them
before a larger audience, perhaps you will accept the dedication
of the volume which contains them.

Faithfully yours,

J. R. LOWELL.

Deerfoot Farm, November 10, 1886.

CONTENTS
  Democracy
  Garfield
  Stanley
  Fielding
  Coleridge
  Books and Libraries
  Wordsworth
  Don Quixote
  Harvard University

DEMOCRACY AND OTHER ADDRESSES. London:
Macmillan, 1887.

DEMOCRACY AND OTHER PAPERS. With Notes.
Boston, *Houghton, Mifflin & Company*, 1898.
18mo, pp. 95, paper, cloth.

  Riverside Literature Series, no. 123.

  CONTENTS
    Democracy
    On a Certain Condescension in Foreigners
    The Study of Modern Languages

DEMOCRACY: AN ESSAY. With an Introductory
Note by Horace E. Scudder. Boston: *Hough-
ton, Mifflin & Co.*, 1902. [March.]
  Limited edition, 16mo, boards.

  NOTICES AND CRITICISMS.
    Nation, "Mr. Lowell's New Volume," December 23, 1886,
      v. 43, p. 525.
    George E. Woodberry, "Mr. Lowell's Addresses," Atlantic
      Monthly, February, 1887, v. 59, p. 257.
    Spectator, February 26, 1887, v. 60, p. 299.
    Walter Lewin, Academy, March 19, 1887, v. 31, p. 196.

  AUCTION SALE PRICES: *On Democracy*, Birmingham, 1884.
    Arnold, January, 1901, $70. Another copy, $110.
    Bangs, November, 1902, $40.
    Bangs, January, 1903, $25.

Peirce, May, 1903, $55.
Somerby, December, 1903, $17.50.
Pattison, October, 1904, $14.
Pyser, February, 1906, $50.
Democracy and Other Addresses.
Anderson, October, 1904, $3.75.
Anderson, April, 1905, $4.50.   Boston, 1886.

BOOKS AND LIBRARIES AND OTHER PAPERS

BOOKS AND LIBRARIES AND OTHER PAPERS. With
  Notes. Boston: *Houghton, Mifflin & Company*,
  1888.
    18mo, pp. 82, paper, cloth.
  Riverside Literature Series, no. 39.

CONTENTS
  Books and Libraries
  Emerson, the Lecturer
  Keats
  Don Quixote

THE INDEPENDENT IN POLITICS

THE INDEPENDENT IN POLITICS.   An Address
  before the Reform Club of New York, April
  13, 1888. [Reform Club Series, – I.]. New
  York: *The Reform Club*, 1888.
    12mo, pp. 27, paper, cloth.

Questions of the Day Series, – no. XLVIII. THE
  INDEPENDENT IN POLITICS. By James Russell Lowell. New York: *Putnams*, 1888.
    12mo, pp. 27, paper, cloth.

AUCTION SALE PRICES.
  Arnold, January, 1901, large paper ed., $14.
  Anderson, January, 1905, $3.85.

POLITICAL ESSAYS

POLITICAL ESSAYS. By James Russell Lowell. [Publishers' vignette.] Boston and New York: *Houghton, Mifflin & Co.*, The Riverside Press, Cambridge, 1888. [July.]

12mo, pp. [vi], 326, cloth.

[iii]   PREFATORY NOTE

I have been often urged to reprint the articles which form the bulk of this volume, by persons who had found them interesting at the time of their first publication, as well as by others who had read them more recently and thought them of some interest even now. I have steadily refused to do what was asked of me, because the greater part of what is here gathered together seemed to me to have mainly a polemic value contemporaneous with the date at which it was written. I have (I know not how wisely) allowed myself to be persuaded that there was also in these papers a certain historical interest as recalling aspects of our politics which perhaps it may be useful not wholly to forget. In looking at them again, after so long an interval (for the latest of them is more than twenty years old), it gratifies me to find so little to regret in their tone, and that I was able to keep my head fairly clear of passion when my heart was at boiling-point.

CONTENTS

POLITICAL ESSAYS. London: *Macmillan*, 1888. Printed at The Riverside Press, new title-page.

NOTICES AND CRITICISMS.

Nation, "Mr. Lowell's Political Philosophy," May 17, 1888, v. 47, p. 111.

Horace E. Scudder, "Mr. Lowell's Politics," Atlantic Monthly, August, 1888, v. 62, p. 274.

Walter Lewin, Academy, August 18, 1888, v. 34, p. 95.

Critic, September 8, 1888, v. 10, p. 111.

HEARTSEASE AND RUE

HEARTSEASE AND RUE. By James Russell Lowell. [Riverside Press vignette.] Boston and New York: *Houghton, Mifflin and Company*, The Riverside Press, Cambridge, 1888. [February.]

16mo, pp. viii, 218, boards and half imitation vellum.

[iii]   Along the wayside where we pass bloom few
       Gay plants of heartsease, more of saddening rue;
       So life is mingled; so should poems be
       That speak a conscious word to you and me.

CONTENTS

A Misconception
The Boss
Sun-worship
Changed Perspective
With a Pair of Gloves lost in a Wager
Sixty-eighth Birthday

THE SAME. London: *Macmillan*, 1888.

Printed at The Riverside Press

NOTICES AND CRITICISMS.

Critic, March 31, 1888, v. 6, p. 150.
Walter Lewin, Academy, March 31, 1888, v. 33, p. 216.
George E. Woodberry, "Mr. Lowell's New Poems,"
  Atlantic Monthly, April, 1888, v. 61, p. 557.
Nation, "Recent Poetry," May 17, 1888, v. 46, p. 406.

AUCTION SALE PRICES. First Edition.

Anderson, May, 1905, with autograph, $32.

LATEST LITERARY ESSAYS AND ADDRESSES

LATEST LITERARY ESSAYS AND ADDRESSES OF
JAMES RUSSELL LOWELL. [Riverside Press
vignette.] Boston and New York: *Houghton,
Mifflin & Co.*, 1892. November, [1891.]
16mo, pp. [vi], 184, cloth, portrait.

[iii]   NOTE

The publication in a volume of the following Essays and Addresses is in accordance with the intention of their author. Most
of them had been revised by him with this end in view. The only
one of them concerning which there is doubt, whether he would
have published it in its present form, is the paper on "Richard
III." With this he was not satisfied, and he hesitated in regard
to printing it. It has seemed to me of interest enough to warrant
its publication.

The essay on Gray was in large part written more than ten
years before it was printed in the "New Princeton Review," in
1880. The essay on the "Areopagitica" was written at the
request of the Grolier Club, of New York, for an introduction to

an edition of the work specially printed for the Club. I am indebted to the Club for permission to include it in this volume.[1]

CHARLES ELIOT NORTON.

Cambridge, Massachusetts,
16 November, 1891.

CONTENTS
Gray
Some Letters of Walter Savage Landor
Walton
Milton's "Areopagitica"
Shakespeare's "Richard III"
The Study of Modern Languages
The Progress of the World

A limited edition of 300 copies was printed from these plates in 1891; portrait on India paper; cloth back, paper label.

NOTICES AND CRITICISMS.
Critic, January 11, 1892, v. 17, p. 31.
Nation, May 12, 1892, v. 54, p. 364.

AUCTION SALE PRICES.
Arnold, January, 1901, large paper ed., $15.
Bangs, December, 1901, large paper ed., $6.25.
French and Chubbuck, February, 1905, $8.
Anderson, April, 1905, Arnold copy, $3.25.

THE OLD ENGLISH DRAMATISTS

THE OLD ENGLISH DRAMATISTS. By James Russell Lowell. [Riverside Press vignette.] Boston and New York: *Houghton, Mifflin and Company.* The Riverside Press, Cambridge, 1892. [November.]

Post 8vo, pp. 132, boards, portrait, 300 printed.

---

[1] The last paragraph first appeared in Elmwood ed.

THE SAME. Boston: *Houghton, Mifflin & Co.*, 1892.

16mo, pp. 132, cloth.

CONTENTS
   i. Introductory
   ii. Marlowe
   iii. Webster
   iv. Chapman
   v. Beaumont and Fletcher
   vi. Massinger and Ford

These lectures were originally published in Harper's Magazine, from June to November, 1892, as follows:

THE OLD ENGLISH DRAMATISTS, June, 1892, v. 85, p. 75.
MARLOWE, July, 1892, v. 85, p. 194.
WEBSTER, August, 1892, v. 85, p. 411.
CHAPMAN, September, 1892, v. 85, p. 561.
BEAUMONT AND FLETCHER, October, 1892, v. 85, p. 757.
MASSINGER AND FORD, November, 1892, v. 85, p. 942.

NOTICES AND CRITICISMS.
Critic, January 7, 1893, v. 19, p. 1.
Dial, February 16, 1896, v. 14, p. 117.

AUCTION SALE PRICES.
French and Chubbuck, February, 1904, large paper ed., $3.25.
Libbie, March, 1904, large paper, $4.50.
Poole, April, 1905, large paper, $3.25.

LETTERS OF JAMES RUSSELL LOWELL

LETTERS OF JAMES RUSSELL LOWELL. Edited by Charles Eliot Norton. Volume i. [Publishers' vignette.] New York: *Harper & Brother*, Publishers, 1894 [1903].

Two volumes, 8vo, pp. viii, 418; 464, cloth, portrait.

[iii]–v   EDITORIAL NOTE

In making the following selection from the great mass of Mr. Lowell's letters which was in my hands, my attempt was to secure for it, so far as possible, an autobiographic character. And, in the main, this has not been difficult, for few writers have given in their letters a more faithful representation of themselves, and of few men is the epistolary record more complete from youth to age. . . .

                         CHARLES ELIOT NORTON.

Shady Hill, Cambridge, Mass.
         July, 1893.

LETTERS OF JAMES RUSSELL LOWELL. Edited by Charles Eliot Norton. In three volumes. Volume I. [Riverside Press vignette.] Boston: *Houghton, Mifflin & Co.*, 1904.

12mo, pp. [x], 348; 409; 370, cloth. Portraits and illustrations, 20 in all.

Appeared in Elmwood, Autograph, and Subscription editions, 1904, enlarged from the ed. of 1894.

"A number of letters, which have come to me since the original edition of this selection of Mr. Lowell's Letters was published, are now included in their respective places in these volumes. They add nothing essential to the image of him presented in the former edition, but serve to fill up some minor parts of its outline with details which strengthen the likeness." — Editor's Note in first volume.

NOTICES AND CRITICISMS.

Charles Eliot Norton, Harper's Magazine, September, 1893, v. 87, p. 553.

Athenæum, October 28, 1893, v. 2, p. 581.

Literary World, November 4, 1893, v. 24, p. 363.

Walter Lewin, Academy, December 9, 1893, v. 44, p. 505.

Thomas Wentworth Higginson, Nation, December 28, 1893, v. 57, p. 488.

J. B. Kenyon, Methodist Review, v. 61, p. 269.

Hamilton Wright Mabie, My Study Fire, second series, 1894.

Horace E. Scudder, Atlantic Monthly, January, 1894, v. 73, p. 124.

Scribner's Magazine, "Mr. Lowell's Letters," January, 1894, v. 15, p. 129.

John White Chadwick, Forum, March, 1894, v. 17, p. 114.

Royal Cortissoz, Century, March, 1897, v. 31, p. 780.

AUCTION SALE PRICES. First Edition.

Arnold, January, 1901, $6.

White, February, 1901, $5.

French and Chubbock, February, 1904, $5.

Libbie, June, 1904, $3.20.

Knapp, February, 1905, $3.

LAST POEMS OF JAMES RUSSELL LOWELL

LAST POEMS OF JAMES RUSSELL LOWELL. [Riverside Press vignette.] Boston and New York: *Houghton, Mifflin and Company*, The Riverside Press, Cambridge. MDCCCXCV. [September, 1895.] [Edited by Professor Charles Eliot Norton.]

12mo, pp. [x], 47, cloth.

CONTENTS

The Oracle of the Goldfishes

Turner's Old Téméraire

St. Michael the Weigher

A Valentine

An April Birthday at Sea

Love and Thought

The Noble Lover

On Hearing a Sonata of Beethoven's played in the next room

Verses

On a Bust of General Grant

[iii] This little volume contains those of the poems which Mr. Lowell wrote in his last years which, I believe, he might have wished to preserve. Three of them were published before his death. Of the rest, two appear for the first time.

September, 1895.   C. E. N.

NOTICES AND CRITICISMS.

Nation, "Recent Poetry," October 24, 1895, v. 61, p. 296.
Athenæum, January 4, 1896, v. 1, p. 12.
M. A. De Wolfe Howe, Atlantic Monthly, February, 1896, v. 77, p. 267.
Dial, February 16, 1896, v. 20 p. 110.

THE POWER OF SOUND

THE POWER OF SOUND: A Rhymed Lecture by James Russell Lowell. Privately printed. New York. MDCCCXCVI.

16mo, pp. x, 35, cloth. The lecture occupies pp. 1–27, notes, 31–35. Reverse of p. 35, stamp of Gillis Press. Number of copy in ink, with initials of E. H. Holden, by whom the publication was made. "Of this Edition of The Power of Sound only seventy-five copies have been printed, of which twenty-five are on Japanese paper and fifty on hand-made."

The editor, Professor Charles Eliot Norton, says in his introductory note: "Mr. Lowell did not esteem this rhymed lecture of sufficient worth to include it in his Published Poems. It is too hasty an improvisation to deserve the *Imprimatur;* but though his judgment of it as a whole would be accepted as correct, it yet contains passages of such excellence, alike of humor and sentiment, and it affords such illustration of his convictions in regard to public affairs just before our Civil War, that, I believe, there can be no question as to the propriety of preserving it in print, and I have therefore acceded with pleasure to Mr. Holden's proposal to print an edition of it for private circulation. I have been unable to ascertain the precise date either of the writing or the delivery of the lecture; nor do I know how often, or, except in a single instance [Newburyport, Mass.], where it was read in public. An approximate date for its original composition, however, and for additions subsequently made to it, may be fixed by internal evidence. There are several references in it to incidents which occurred during the summer of 1857, from which it may be concluded that it was written in the autumn or early winter of that year; while other references in the additions show that the latest of them belong to the spring of 1862. The only existing copy of the poem is in print on galley slips, cut up so as to make twenty-three pages. The margins of many of these pages are full of corrections and additions written in ink or pencil. It was put into type and cut up into its present form for convenience of reading in public."

Auction Sale Prices.

Roos, April, 1897, $26.

LECTURES ON ENGLISH POETS

Lectures on English Poets. By James Russell Lowell.

> — "Call up him who left half-told
> The story of Cambuscan bold."

Cleveland. The Rowfant Club, mdcccxcvii. 8vo, boards.

Reprinted from the Boston Daily Advertiser for January and February, 1855.

Lowell's Lectures before the Lowell Institute were reported in the Boston Daily Advertiser, as follows:

   i. Definitions, Wednesday, January 10, 1855.
   ii. Piers Ploughman's Vision, Saturday, January 13.
  iii. The Metrical Romances, Wednesday, January 17.
   iv. The Ballads, Saturday, January 20.
   v. Chaucer, Wednesday, January 24.
   vi. Spenser, Saturday, January 27.
  vii. Milton, Wednesday, January 31.
 viii. Butler, Saturday, February 3.
   ix. Pope, Wednesday, February 7.
   x. Poetic Diction, Saturday, February 10.
   xi. Wordsworth, Wednesday, February 14.
  xii. [Poetry,] Saturday, February 17.

Auction Sale Prices.
  Libbie, February, 1900, $12.50.
  Mackay, April, 1900, $13.50.
  Arnold, January, 1901, $30.
  French, April, 1901, $18.
  Anderson, April, 1903, $22.

IMPRESSIONS OF SPAIN

Impressions of Spain. James Russell Lowell. Compiled by Joseph B. Gilder. With an Introduction by A. A. Adee. Boston and New York: *Houghton, Mifflin & Co.*, The Riverside Press, 1899. [November.]
  12mo, pp. ix, 107, boards, vellum back.
  Prefatory Note, iii–vii. Introduction, 3–19.

vii. "The letters which have been chosen for reproduction here are those in which our Minister describes the domestic politics of Spain; the King's first marriage, at the age of twenty-one, to his cousin Mercedes; the attempt upon his life; his bereavement; and his marriage to the Austrian Archduchess, Maria Cristina."

Contents
  The Domestic Politics of Spain
  The King's First Marriage
  The Death of Queen Mercedes
  Attempted Assassination of the King
  General Grant's Visit to Spain
  The King's Second Marriage

Most of the letters contained in this volume were originally published by the State Department in Executive Documents vol. i, 1878. They were partly reprinted in The Critic for September, 1898, and The Century for November, 1898.

Notices and Criticisms.
  Academy, February 10, 1900, v. 58, p. 124.

THE ANTI–SLAVERY PAPERS OF JAMES RUSSELL LOWELL

THE ANTI-SLAVERY PAPERS OF JAMES RUS-
SELL LOWELL, I. [Riverside Press vignette.]
Boston and New York: *Houghton, Mifflin
& Co.* MDCCCCII. [November.]

Two volumes, 8vo, pp. xiii, 223; 203, boards.
Edition limited to 500.

Edited by William Belmont Parker, who wrote the
introduction, pp. [v]–ix.

"Most of the papers included in these two volumes are re-
printed from the original manuscripts, now in the hands of
Mrs. Sydney Howard Gay." They appeared originally in the
"Pennsylvania Freeman" and in the "National Anti-Slavery
Journal."

CONTENTS OF VOL. I
  A Word in Season
  Texas
  The Prejudice of Color
  The Church and Clergy
  The Church and Clergy Again
  Daniel Webster
  The French Revolution of 1848
  Shall We Ever Be Republican?
  Presidential Candidates
  An Imaginary Conversation
  The Sacred Parasol
  The Nominations for the Presidency
  Sympathy with Ireland
  What will Mr. Webster do?
  The News from Paris
  The Buffalo Convention
  The Irish Rebellion
  Fanaticism in the Navy
  Exciting Intelligence from South Carolina Turncoats.

NOTICES AND CRITICISMS.

    Scribner's Magazine, "Mr. Lowell in Anti-Slavery Days," November, 1891, v. 10, p. 657.

    Nation, "Lowell the Reformer," January 1, 1903, v. 76, p. 14.

    William Rice, Dial, "Lowell on Human Liberty," January 1, 1903, v. 34, p. 14.

AUCTION SALE PRICES.

    French and Chubbuck, February, 1904, $7.

    Anderson, May, 1904, $5.50.

    Anderson, October, 1904, $6.

    Darrah, November, 1904, $3.25.

    McCormack, February, 1905, $3.75.

    Libbie, March, 1905, $3.50.

    Anderson, April, 1905, $6.50.

    Libbie, May, 1905, $5.50.

EARLY WRITINGS OF JAMES RUSSELL LOWELL

EARLY WRITINGS OF JAMES RUSSELL LOWELL. With a Prefatory Note by Dr. Hale, and an Introduction by Walter Littlefield. Published by *John Lane*, The Bodley Head, London and New York. [September, 1902.]

Crown 8vo, pp. xxxviii, 248, boards, cloth back. Portrait.

CONTENTS

    Stories, Sketches, Essays

      The First Client

      Married Men

      Getting up

      Disquisition on Foreheads

      Song-writing

    Elizabethan Dramatists, omitting Shakespeare

      George Chapman

      John Webster

John Ford
Philip Massinger
Thomas Middleton

NOTICES AND CRITICISMS.

Nation, November 27, 1902, v. 75, p. 429.
Academy, "The Beginnings of an Author," January 17, 1903,
v. 64, p. 65.

COLLECTED POEMS

THE POETICAL WORKS OF JAMES RUSSELL LOW-
ELL. Complete in Two Volumes. Boston:
Ticknor and Fields, 1858 [1857].

Blue and Gold edition. 32mo, pp. ix, 315;
xi, 322; blue cloth, gilt edges. Portrait.

[v] This volume, originally inscribed with his name, fourteen
years ago, is re-dedicated, with still-renewing affection, to
William Page, in Rome.

CONTENTS OF VOL. I
Miscellaneous Poems
Threnodia
The Sirens
Irené
Serenade
With a Pressed Flower
The Beggar
My Love
Summer Storm
Love
To Perdita, singing
The Moon
Remembered Music
Song: to M. L.
Allegra
The Fountain
Ode
The Fatherland
The Forlorn

Sonnets

This was the first complete edition of Lowell's Poetical Works. The early poems were grouped as "Miscellaneous," the "Memorial Verses" placed together, while the sonnets were arranged as in all subsequent editions.

The second volume was dedicated: "To Charles F. Briggs this volume is affectionately inscribed."

THE SAME.

16mo edition from same plates, 1877.

AUCTION SALE PRICES.

Foote, November, 1894, $7.

THE POETICAL WORKS OF JAMES RUSSELL LOW-
ELL. Complete Edition. [Publishers' mono-
gram.] Boston: *Fields, Osgood & Co.*, 1869.
[November.]
    18mo, pp. ix, 437, double columns, cloth.

[iii] To George William Curtis, this first complete edition of
    my poems is affectionately inscribed.

CONTENTS
    Miscellaneous Poems
    Memorial Verses
    Sonnets
    The Vision of Sir Launfal
    A Fable for Critics
    The Biglow Papers, First Series
    The Biglow Papers, Second Series
    The Unhappy Lot of Mr. Knott
    An Oriental Apologue
    Under the Willows, and Other Poems
    Poems of the War
    L'Envoi: To the Muse

THE SAME. Cabinet Edition. Two volumes.
Boston: *Ticknor & Fields*, 1864. [October.]
    16mo, garnet cloth. Same as Blue and Gold
Edition.

POETICAL WORKS, including A Fable for Critics.
Preface by W. B. B. Stevens. London, 1865.
    8vo.

THE POETICAL WORKS OF JAMES RUSSELL LOW-
ELL. Complete edition. With Illustrations.
Boston: *Fields, Osgood & Co.*, 1870. [Decem-
ber.]
    16mo, pp. 437, cloth. Portrait.

CONTENTS
    Miscellaneous Poems
    Memorial Verses
    Sonnets
    The Vision of Sir Launfal
    A Fable for Critics
    The Biglow Papers, Both Series
    The Unhappy Lot of Mr. Knott
    An Oriental Apologue
    Under the Willows, and Other Poems
    Poems of the War
    L'Envoi: To the Muse
    The Cathedral

THE SAME. Diamond Edition.
    18mo.

THE SAME. Red-line Edition.
    Small 4to, full gilt; portrait and cuts.

THE SAME. Household Edition.
    12mo.

THE SAME. New Revised Edition. With numerous illustrations. [Publishers' monogram.] Boston: *James R. Osgood and Company*, late *Ticknor & Fields, and Fields, Osgood & Co.*, 1877. [1876.]
    8vo, pp. xii, 406, cloth. Portrait.
CONTENTS
    Earlier Poems
        Threnodia
        The Sirens
        Irené
        Serenade
        With a Pressed Flower
        The Beggar
        My Love

In this edition the poems were carefully revised, many excisions made, and the separation made into "Earlier" and "Miscellaneous."

THE SAME. Illustrated Library Edition, October, 1876, as above.

THE SAME. Household Edition, August, 1876. 12mo.

THE SAME. Critical Preface by William Michael Rossetti. London, Moxon's Popular Poets, 1880.
12mo and 8vo, pp. xvi, 623.

THE SAME. Revised edition, with illustrations. London: *Routledge*, November, 1881.
8vo, pp. xii, 422.

THE SAME. London: Routledge's Excelsior Series, 1884.
Pp. 512.

THE SAME. New edition. London: *Macmillan*, July, 1880.
12mo.

THE SAME. London: *Ward and Lock*, October, 1880.
Post 8vo.

THE SAME. Illustrated Household Edition. Boston: *Houghton, Mifflin & Co.*, June, 1885.

POEMS. Library Edition, new size. Boston: *Houghton, Mifflin & Co.*, 1886.

THE SAME. Family Edition. Boston: *Houghton, Mifflin & Co.*, July, 1887.

HOUSEHOLD EDITION. Complete Poetical Works.
Boston: *Houghton, Mifflin & Co.*, 1895.
  Crown 8vo, pp. xvii, 515. Portrait; illus-
trations. Red cloth, gilt top.

CONTENTS
  [Biographical Sketch, by Horace E. Scudder]
  Earlier Poems
  Sonnets
  Miscellaneous Poems
  Memorial Verses
  The Vision of Sir Launfal
  A Fable for Critics
  Letter from Boston
  The Biglow Papers, First and Second Series
  The Unhappy Lot of Mr. Knott
  An Oriental Apologue
  Fragments of an Unfinished Poem
  Under the Willows, and Other Poems
  Poems of the War
  The Cathedral
  Three Memorial Poems
  Heartsease and Rue
  Last Poems
  Index of First Lines
  Index of Titles

THE COMPLETE POETICAL WORKS OF JAMES
RUSSELL LOWELL. Cambridge Edition. [Illus-
tration of Elmwood, Cambridge.] Boston and
New York: *Houghton, Mifflin & Co.* The
Riverside Press, Cambridge. [February, 1897;
copyright, 1896.]

  Large crown 8vo, pp. xvii, 492, gilt top,
brown cloth. Portrait; engraved title with
vignette of Lowell's home; notes and introductions by Horace E. Scudder.

Contents

LIBRARY EDITION. Complete Poetical Works. Same as Household Edition.

8vo, gilt top. Portrait ; 16 photogravures.

CABINET EDITION. Complete Poetical Works, 1899.

COLLECTED WORKS

RIVERSIDE EDITION. The Writings of James Russell Lowell. In Ten Volumes. [Riverside Press Vignette.] Boston and New York, *Houghton, Mifflin and Company,* The Riverside Press, Cambridge, MDCCCXC.

16mo, brown cloth; portraits.

Vol. I. LITERARY ESSAYS, I

PREFATORY NOTE TO THE ESSAYS

[v] The greater part of the literary and critical essays here collected was originally written as lectures for an audience consisting not only of my own classes but also of such other members of the university as might choose to attend them. This will account for, if it do not excuse, a more rhetorical tone in them here and there than I should have allowed myself had I been writing for the eye and not the ear. They were meant to be suggestive of certain broader principles of criticism based on the comparative study of literature in its large meaning, rather than methodically pedagogic, to stimulate rather than to supply the place of individual study. . . .

[vi] Let me add that in preparing these papers for the press I omitted much illustrative and subsidiary matter, and this I regret when it is too late. Five or six lectures, for instance, were condensed into the essay on Rousseau. The dates attached were those of publication, but the bulk of the material was written many years earlier, some of it so long ago as 1854. . . .

25th April, 1890.   J. R. L.

CONTENTS

Vol. VI. LITERARY AND POLITICAL ADDRESSES

CONTENTS

Vol. VII. POEMS, I

[iii]   PREFATORY NOTE TO THE POEMS

There are a great many pieces in these volumes, especially in the first of them, which I would gladly suppress or put into the Coventry of smaller print in an appendix. But "ilka mon maun dree his weird," and the avenging *litera scripta manet* is that of an overhasty author. Owing to the unjust distinction made by the law between literary and other property, most of what I published prematurely has lost the protection of copyright, and is reprinted by others against my will. I cannot shake off the burden of my early indiscretions if I would. The best way, perhaps, is to accept with silent contrition the consequences of one's own mistakes, and I have, after much hesitation, consented to the reprinting of the old editions without excision.

I must confess, however, that I have attained this pitch of self-sacrifice only by compulsion, and should have greatly preferred to increase the value of this collection by lessening its bulk. The judicious reader will, I fear, distinguish only too easily what I should wish, in parliamentary phrase, "to be taken as read." ...

CONTENTS
Earlier Poems
Sonnets
Miscellaneous Poems
Memorial Verses
The Vision of Sir Launfal
Letter from Boston, December, 1846

VOL. VIII. POEMS, II

CONTENTS
The Biglow Papers, First Series
The Biglow Papers, Second Series

VOL. IX. POEMS, III

CONTENTS
A Fable for Critics
The Unhappy Lot of Mr. Knott
Fragments of an Unpublished Poem
An Oriental Apologue
Under the Willows, and Other Poems

VOL. X. POEMS, IV

CONTENTS
Poems of the War
L'Envoi
The Cathedral
Three Memorial Poems
Heartsease and Rue
Index of First Lines
General Index of Titles

Edition of vol. IV, 1897, adds The Last Poems, increasing pages to 298.
In 1892 a prose volume was added to this edition, and numbered.

VOL. XI. LATEST LITERARY ESSAYS AND ADDRESSES.
Editorial Note by Charles Eliot Norton. [November, 1892.]

[156]

Contents

A Large Paper Edition also was published in 1890.

STANDARD LIBRARY EDITION. Writings. Ten volumes, September, 1891. Illustrated with 83 steel engravings and photogravures.

This edition is printed from the plates of the Riverside Edition and the contents of the different volumes are unchanged. The set was increased by the addition of volume xi, in 1892; and when the two volumes of Mr. Scudder's Biography of Lowell were issued, in 1902, they also were included in the Standard Library Edition.

POPULAR EDITION. Boston, *Houghton, Mifflin & Co.*, 1892.
  12mo.

Vol. I. Fireside Travels
Vol. II. Among My Books, First Series
Vol. III. Among My Books, Second Series

Vol. IV. My Study Windows
Vol. V. Political Essays
Vol. VI. Poetical Works

ELMWOOD EDITION. The Complete Writings of James Russell Lowell. In Sixteen Volumes. Boston: *Houghton, Mifflin and Company*, The Riverside Press, Cambridge, 1904.

12mo, green cloth, gilt top. Portraits, illustrations, facsimiles. [86 in all.]

"This edition varies from the Riverside edition of 1890 in the retention of the original titles of the volumes of prose essays." — Publishers' Note, vol. i.

Vol. I. FIRESIDE TRAVELS
[iii] Publishers' Note
CONTENTS
Introduction [by Bliss Perry]
Cambridge Thirty Years Ago
A Moosehead Journal
Leaves from My Journal in Italy and Elsewhere
    I. At Sea
    II. In the Mediterranean
    III. Italy
    IV. A Few Bits of Roman Mosaic
My Garden Acquaintance
On a Certain Condescension in Foreigners
A Good Word for Winter

Vol. II. MY STUDY WINDOWS
CONTENTS
A Great Public Character
Carlyle
The Life and Letters of James Gates Percival
Thoreau
Swinburne's Tragedies
Chaucer
Library of Old Authors
Emerson the Lecturer
Pope

Vol. III. Among My Books. First and Second Series, i

Contents
Dryden
Witchcraft
Shakespeare Once More

Vol. IV. Among My Books. First and Second Series, ii

Contents
New England Two Centuries Ago
Lessing
Rousseau and the Sentimentalists
Spenser

Vol. V. Among My Books. First and Second Series, iii

Contents
Dante
Wordsworth
Milton
Keats

Vol. VI. Political Essays

Contents
The American Tract Society
The Election in November
E Pluribus Unum
The Pickens-and-Stealin's Rebellion
General McClellan's Report
The Rebellion; Its Causes and Consequences
McClellan or Lincoln?
Abraham Lincoln
Reconstruction
Scotch the Snake, or Kill it?
The President on the Stump
The Seward-Johnson Reaction

Vol. VII. Literary and Political Addresses

Contents
Democracy
Garfield
Stanley

VOL. VIII. LATEST LITERARY ESSAYS. THE OLD ENGLISH DRAMATISTS

Vol. IX. THE POETICAL WORKS OF JAMES RUSSELL LOWELL, I

VOL. X. POETICAL WORKS, II
The Biglow Papers, First Series.

VOL. XI. POETICAL WORKS, III
The Biglow Papers, Second Series.

VOL. XII. POETICAL WORKS, IV
CONTENTS
A Fable for Critics
The Unhappy Lot of Mr. Knott
Fragments of an Unfinished Poem
An Oriental Apologue
Under the Willows, and Other Poems

VOL. XIII. POETICAL WORKS. V
CONTENTS
Poems of the War
The Cathedral
Three Memorial Poems
Heartsease and Rue
Last Poems
Index of First Lines
General Index of Titles

VOL. XIV. LETTERS OF JAMES RUSSELL LOWELL. Edited by Charles Eliot Norton, I.

[iii] Note of the Editor. "A number of letters which have come to me since the original edition of this selection of Mr. Lowell's Letters was published, are now included in their respective places in these volumes."

VOL. XV. LETTERS, II

VOL. XVI. LETTERS, III

AUTOGRAPH EDITION. The Complete Writings of James Russell Lowell. In Sixteen Volumes. Boston: *Houghton, Mifflin and Company*, 1904. Large Paper Edition, printed from the plates of the Elmwood Edition. Limited to 1000 numbered copies.

SELECTIONS AND COMPILATIONS[1]

MY GARDEN ACQUAINTANCE, etc. Boston: *Houghton, Mifflin and Company*, 1871.
32mo, pp. 95, cloth. Illustrated.
Modern Classics, no. 31.

CONTENTS
My Garden Acquaintance
A Good Word for Winter
A Moosehead Journal
At Sea

LOWELL BIRTHDAY BOOK. Boston: *Houghton, Mifflin & Co.*, February, 1883.
18mo, pp. 402, cloth. Portrait and illustrations.

THE SAME. London: *Chatto*, 1883. 32mo.

LOWELL CALENDAR FOR 1886. Boston: *Houghton, Mifflin & Co.*, May, 1885.

LOWELL CALENDAR FOR 1887. Boston: *Houghton, Mifflin & Co.*, August, 1886.

LOWELL CALENDAR FOR 1889. Boston: *Houghton, Mifflin & Co.*, August, 1887.

LOWELL CALENDAR FOR 1890. Boston: *Houghton, Mifflin & Co.*, September, 1889.

[1] See also the list of separate works, where several volumes of selections, taking their titles from the initial poems, are listed.

LOWELL BIRTHDAY BOOK. London: *Warne*, 1898.
16mo.

UNDER THE OLD ELM, AND OTHER POEMS. With
Notes and a Biographical Sketch. Boston:
Houghton, Mifflin & Co., 1885.
18mo, pp. 96, cloth.
Riverside Literature Series, no. 15.

CONTENTS
Biographical Sketch
Under the Old Elm
Ode read at Concord
Under the Willows
Cochituate Ode
The Courtin'
To H. W. Longfellow
Agassiz
To Holmes
To Whittier
An Incident in a Railroad Car
The Fountain
An Ember Picture
Phœbe
To the Dandelion
She came and went
Yussouf
The Maple
Appendix. In the Laboratory with Agassiz, by a former
Pupil.

THE ENGLISH POETS, LESSING, ROUSSEAU.
Essays by James Russell Lowell, with "An
Apology for a Preface." London: *Walter Scott*,
1888.
16mo, pp. x, 337, cloth. Preface to this
edition, by Lowell, pp. vii–x.
The Camelot Series. Edited by Ernest Rhys.

CONTENTS
  Spenser
  Shakespeare Once More
  Milton
  Wordsworth
  Keats
  Lessing
  Rousseau and the Sentimentalists

AMERICAN IDEAS FOR ENGLISH READERS. By
James Russell Lowell. With Introduction by
Henry Stone. Published by *J. G. Cupples Co.*,
Boston. [1892.]
  Narrow 16mo, pp. xv, 94, cloth.
  An unauthorized reprint of newspaper reports of lectures and addresses delivered in England.

CONTENTS
  Before the Edinburgh Philosophical Institution
  Before the London Chamber of Commerce
  At the University of Cambridge
  On Robert Browning
  At the Unveiling of the Gray Memorial
  Before the Town Council of the City of Worcester
  On International Arbitration
  At a Royal Academy Dinner
  At the Stratford Memorial Fountain Presentation
  At the Dinner to American Authors
  Before the Liverpool Philomathic Society

ODES, LYRICS, AND SONNETS. Boston: *Houghton, Mifflin & Co.*, 1892. [November, 1891.]
  16mo, 193 pp., cloth.

CONTENTS
  Odes
    Ode recited at the Harvard Commemoration, July 21,
      1865
    Agassiz
    Under the Old Elm

Lowell Leaflets: Poems and Prose Passages.
Compiled by Josephine E. Hodgdon. Boston:
Houghton, Mifflin & Co., 1896.
Crown 8vo, pp. 102, cloth.
Riverside Literature Series, no. 99, extra.

Contents

Nature, by Ralph Waldo Emerson. MY GARDEN
ACQUAINTANCE. By James Russell Lowell.
Prescribed by the Regents of the University of

the State of New York for the Course in American Selections, Introduction, Biographical Sketch of Emerson, and Notes to Both Essays. Boston: *Houghton, Mifflin & Co.*, 1902.

18mo, pp. 78, cloth.

Riverside Literature Series, no. 149, extra (T).

CONTENTS

Introduction
Emerson's Career
Nature. By Ralph Waldo Emerson
My Garden Acquaintance. By James Russell Lowell
Notes

THE CHIEF AMERICAN POETS: Selected Poems by Bryant, Poe, Emerson, Longfellow, Whittier, Holmes, Lowell, Whitman, and Lanier. Edited, with notes, reference lists, and biographical sketches, by Curtis Hidden Page. Boston: *Houghton, Mifflin and Company*, 1905.

8vo, xii, 713 pp. Lowell, pp. 410–531.

CONTENTS [Selections from Lowell]

"For this true nobleness I seek in vain "
My Love
"My Love, I have no fear that thou shouldst die"
"I ask not for those thoughts, that sudden leap"
"Great Truths are portions of the soul of man"
To the Spirit of Keats
"Our Love is not a fading, earthly flower"
"Beloved, in the noisy city here"
Song: "O Moonlight deep and tender"
The Shepherd of King Admetus
An Incident in a Railroad Car
Stanzas on Freedom
Wendell Phillips
Rhœcus
To the Dandelion

WORKS EDITED BY LOWELL

In the case of the first six works listed under this heading the biographical introduction was contributed or edited by Lowell and the text was printed under his care.

THE POETICAL WORKS OF JOHN KEATS. With a Life. Boston: *Little, Brown and Company.* New York: *Evans and Dickerson.* Philadelphia: *Lippincott, Grambo & Co.* M.DCCC.LIV.

The Life of Keats, pp. vii–xxxvi.

THE POETICAL WORKS OF JOHN DRYDEN. Boston: *Little, Brown and Company.* New York: *Evans and Dickerson.* Philadelphia: *Lippincott, Grambo and Co.* M.DCCC.LIV.

In five volumes.

THE POETICAL WORKS OF WILLIAM WORDSWORTH, D. C. L., Poet Laureate, etc., etc. Boston: *Little, Brown and Company.* New York: *Evans and Dickerson.* Philadelphia: *Lippincott, Grambo, and Co.* M.DCCC.LIV.

In six volumes. Sketch of Wordsworth's Life, vol. I, pp. viii–xl.

THE POETICAL WORKS OF PERCY BYSSHE SHELLEY. Edited by Mrs. Shelley. With a Memoir. Boston: *Little, Brown and Company.* New York: *James S. Dickerson.* Philadelphia: *Lippincott, Grambo and Co.* M.DCCC.LV.

Lui non trov' io, ma suoi santi vestigi
Tutti rivolti alla superna strada
Veggio, lunge da' laghi averni e stigi.   — PETRARCA.

In three volumes.

THE POETICAL WORKS OF DR. JOHN DONNE.
With a Memoir. Boston: *Little, Brown and
Company. Shepard, Clark and Co.* New York:
James S. Dickerson. Philadelphia: *J. B. Lip-
pincott and Co.* M.DCCC.LV.

Some account of the Life of Dr. John Donne, pp.
xi–xiv.

THE POETICAL WORKS OF ANDREW MARVELL.
With a Memoir of the Author. Boston: *Little,
Brown and Company. Shepherd, Clark and
Brown.* Cincinnati: *Moore, Wilstach, Keys and
Co.* M.DCCC.LVII.

Notice of the Author, pp. ix–liii.

IL PESCEBALLO. Opera Seria: In un Atto, Mu-
sica del Maestro Rossibelli-Donimosarti. The
words by F. J. Child, the English text by
Lowell. Cambridge: Privately printed, 1862.

16mo, pp. 31, paper.

Presented in Boston, 1861, 1862. In 1862 at Horti-
cultural Hall, May 10, 12,14, for the benefit of the people
of East Tennessee.

AUCTION SALE PRICES.
French and Chubbuck, February, 1904, $25.
Anderson, January, 1904, $24.
Anderson, January, 1905, $79.
Knapp, February, 1905, $18.

THE SAME. Chicago: *Caxton Club,* 1899.

8vo, paper.

THE HARVARD BOOK. A Series of Historical, Biographical, and Descriptive Sketches. By Various Authors. Illustrated. By F. O. Vaille and H. A. Clark. Cambridge, 1875.

> In two volumes.
>
> "Class Day," by Lowell, vol. ii, pp. 157–172.

TRUE MANLINESS. Thomas Hughes. Edited by E. E. Brown. Introduction by James Russell Lowell. Boston: *D. Lothrop & Co.*, 1880.

> Spare Minute Series.

BIRMINGHAM HEALTH LECTURES. Second Series. Preface by James Russell Lowell. Birmingham: *Hudson & Son*, 1883.

THE PROGRESS OF THE WORLD. Introduction by James Russell Lowell. Boston: *Gately & O'Gorman*, 1886.

> Reprinted in Latest Literary Essays, 1891.

THE COMPLETE ANGLER, or the Contemplative Man's Recreation, of Isaak Walton and Charles Cotton, with an Introduction by James Russell Lowell. [Edited by John Bartlett.] Boston: *Little, Brown & Co.*, 1889.

> In two volumes.
>
> Lowell's Introduction, pp. xv–lxv. Reprinted in Latest Literary Essays, 1891.

JOHN MILTON. AREOPAGITICA. A Speech for the Liberty of Unlicensed Printing, to the Parliament of England. With an Introduction by

James Russell Lowell. New York: *The Grolier Club*, 1890.

16mo, pp. lvii, 189. Portrait. Edition of 325 copies.

POEMS. JOHN DONNE. From the Text of the Edition of 1633, revised by James Russell Lowell. With the various readings of the other editions of the Seventeenth Century, and with a preface, an introduction, and notes by Charles Eliot Norton. New York: *The Grolier Club*, 1895.

In two volumes.

"After the publication of the Boston edition [1855], Mr. Lowell scored the margins of the volume with emendations, mainly of the punctuation, amounting to many hundreds in number. It seemed a pity that this work should be lost, and the Grolier Club undertook the present edition for the sake of preserving it. In order to give this issue still further value, a comparison has been made of the texts of all of the editions of the seventeenth century, from the first in 1633 to the last in 1669, and the various readings noted. This was done by Mrs. Burnett, the daughter of Mr. Lowell, and by myself, with the result which is shown in the footnotes."

ADDRESSES AND SPEECHES

TRIBUTE TO JOHN P. KENNEDY, at the meeting of the
Massachusetts Historical Society held September, 1870.
Proceedings, v. 11, p. 365.

SPEECH ON WASHINGTON ANNIVERSARY IN CAMBRIDGE.
Proceedings, July 3, 1875, in Celebration of the Centennial Anniversary of Washington's taking Command
of the Continental Army at Cambridge Common.
Cambridge, 1875, 8vo, cloth.

TRIBUTE TO EDMUND QUINCY, at the meeting of the Massachusetts Historical Society held June, 1877.
Proceedings, v. 17, p. 286.

SPEECH IN MEMORIAL HALL on the Old South Meeting-
House.
Report of a Meeting of the Inhabitants of Cambridge
in Memorial Hall, Harvard College, January 18, 1877.
Boston, Press of George H. Ellis, 1877. 8vo.

SPEECH AT A DINNER given him by the directors of the Edinburgh Philosophical Institution, Balmoral Hotel, Edinburgh, November 6, 1880.
American Ideas for English Readers, 1892.

SPEECH AT SAVAGE CLUB Déjeuner to American Actors.
Reported in The Era, London, August 2, 1880.

ADDRESS ON GARFIELD'S DEATH.
Death of President Garfield. Meeting of Americans
in London, at Exeter Hall, 24 September, 1881. Address
by Lowell. London, *Benjamin Franklin Stevens*, Chis-

wick Press, 1881. Square 12mo, linen. 100 copies
printed. Introduction by Lowell.

> Democracy, and Other Addresses, 1886. Contains both
introduction and address.

SPEECH AT DINNER, LONDON CHAMBER OF COMMERCE,
January 29, 1883.

> American Ideas for English Readers, 1892.

ADDRESS ON UNVEILING THE BUST OF FIELDING, delivered
at Shire Hall, Taunton, Somersetshire, September 4,
1883.

> Democracy, and Other Addresses, 1886.

SPEECH AT THE MEETING IN THE CHAPTER HOUSE OF WEST-
MINSTER ABBEY IN COMMEMORATION OF DEAN STANLEY,
December 13, 1881.

> Democracy, and Other Addresses, 1886.

ADDRESS READ BEFORE THE EDINBURGH PHILOSOPHICAL
INSTITUTION, 1883, on Shakespeare's "Richard III."

> Atlantic Monthly, December, 1891, v. 68, p. 816.
> Latest Literary Essays and Addresses, 1891.

ADDRESS BEFORE THE UNION LEAGUE CLUB OF CHICAGO,
December, 1886, on Shakespeare's "Richard III."

ADDRESS AT THE UNIVERSITY OF CAMBRIDGE ON THE
OPENING OF ARCHÆOLOGICAL BUILDINGS, May 6, 1884.

> American Ideas for English Readers, 1892.

SPEECH AT DULWICH COLLEGE.

> Reported in London Times.

LETTER ON A MAJOR IN BRITISH ARMY.

> Proceedings of the Massachusetts Historical Society.
> Second Series, vol. 1, p. 229. Boston, 1884. 8vo.

DESPATCH TO STATE DEPARTMENT.
>Proceedings of the Massachusetts Historical Society. Second Series, vol. 11, p. 208.

ADDRESS ON BROWNING at the twenty-fourth meeting of the London Browning Society, April 25, 1884.
>Browning Society Papers, Part v, p. 112, 1884.
>American Ideas for English Readers, 1892.

ADDRESS AS PRESIDENT OF THE WORDSWORTH SOCIETY, May 10, 1884.
>Report of the Fifth Annual Meeting. Transactions of the Wordsworth Society. No. vi. Edinburgh, *Constable*, 1884.
>Wordsworthiana: a Selection from Papers read to the Wordsworth Society. Edited by William Knight. London, *Macmillan*, 1889.
>Democracy, and Other Addresses, 1888.

BIRMINGHAM AND MIDLAND INSTITUTE. ON DEMOCRACY: an address delivered in the Town Hall, Birmingham, on the 6th of October, 1884. By his Excellency, the Hon. James Russell Lowell, D.C.L., LL.D., American Minister in London, President. Birmingham: Printed by *Cond Bros.*, Paternoster Row, Moor Street, 1884. This first edition differs from the following.
>Pall Mall Gazette, October 10, 1884, pp. 13–15.
>London edition, 1884, 8vo. Cambridge edition, 1902, 12mo, boards.
>Democracy, and Other Addresses, 1886.

ADDRESS ON UNVEILING THE BUST OF COLERIDGE, in Westminster Abbey, May 7, 1885.
>Democracy, and Other Addresses, 1886.

ADDRESS BEFORE THE TOWN COUNCIL OF THE CITY OF WORCESTER, in reply to an address presented to him by the Mayor on behalf of the citizens, June 2, 1885.
>American Ideas for English Readers, 1892.

ADDRESS ON INTERNATIONAL ARBITRATION TO A DEPUTATION FROM THE WORKMEN'S PEACE ASSOCIATION, which waited on Mr. Lowell at the official residence in Albemarle Street, on the evening of June 6, 1884.
American Ideas for English Readers, 1892.

ADDRESS DELIVERED ON THE OCCASION OF THE UNVEILING OF THE BUST OF THE POET GRAY, in the hall of Pembroke College, Cambridge, May 26, 1885.
American Ideas for English Readers, 1892.

SPEECH ON CONCORD IN LITERATURE.
Celebration of the 250th Anniversary of the Incorporation of Concord, September 12, 1885. Concord, 1885, 8vo.

ADDRESS ON BOOKS AND LIBRARIES.
Proceedings at the Dedication of the New Library Building, Chelsea, Mass., December 22, 1885. [With the Address by James Russell Lowell on Books and Libraries.] Cambridge, *John Wilson and Son*, University Press, 1886, 8vo, paper.
Boston Daily Advertiser, December 23, 1885.
Democracy, and Other Addresses, 1886.

NOTES ON DON QUIXOTE, read at the Workingmen's College, Great Ormond Street, London. (1885?)
Democracy, and Other Addresses, 1886.

ADDRESSES AT THE INAUGURATION OF BRYN MAWR COLLEGE, 1885. Philadelphia, 1886, 8vo. Address by Lowell.

ADDRESS ON "LITERATURE" at the annual dinner of the Royal Academy held at Burlington House, London, May 3, 1886.
American Ideas for English Readers, 1892.

ADDRESS ON DANTE.

Fifth Annual Report of the Dante Society, May 16, 1886. Cambridge, 1886, 8vo.

ADDRESS ON FOUNDING OF HARVARD UNIVERSITY.

A Record of the Commemoration, Nov. 5th to 8th, 1886, on the Two Hundred and Fiftieth Anniversary of the Founding of Harvard University. 8vo, Cambridge, 1887.

Atlantic Monthly, December, 1886. Supplement I. Oration of James Russell Lowell, and the Poem of Oliver Wendell Holmes, delivered in Sanders Theatre, Cambridge, November 8, 1886, on the two hundred and fiftieth anniversary of the foundation.

Democracy, and Other Addresses, 1886.

TRIBUTE TO CHARLES FRANCIS ADAMS at the meeting of the Massachusetts Historical Society held in December, 1886.

Proceedings, second series, v. 3, p. 149.

ADDRESS AT ANNIVERSARY OF WEST CHURCH.

The West Church, Boston. Commemorative Services on the Fiftieth Anniversary of its Present Ministry and One Hundred and Fiftieth of its Foundation, March 1, 1887. Boston, 1887, 8vo.

ADDRESS ON INTERNATIONAL COPYRIGHT in Chickering Hall, New York, November 28, 1887. Lowell presided at Author's Reading, read two of his short poems, and gave address.

The Critic, "Lowell's Address on International Copyright," December 3, 1887, v. 8, p. 281.

SPEECH FROM THE CHAIR AT THE MEETING FOR THE FORMATION OF THE INTERNATIONAL COPYRIGHT ASSOCIATION, December 27, 1887.

Proceedings, Boston, 1888, 8vo.

ADDRESS AT A MEETING OF THE TARIFF REFORM LEAGUE, Boston, December 29, 1887.

Literary and Political Addresses, 1890.

THE INDEPENDENT IN POLITICS. An address delivered before the Reform Club of New York [at Steinway Hall], April 13, 1888.

Reform Club Series. I. New York, The Reform Club, 1888. Pp. 27. 8vo, paper.

Questions of the Day Series, no. 48. *Putnams*, New York, pp. 27, 12mo, 1888.

New York Evening Post, April 17, 1888.

Literary and Political Addresses, 1890.

REPORT OF THE PROCEEDINGS AT THE DINNER GIVEN BY THE SOCIETY OF AUTHORS TO AMERICAN MEN AND WOMEN OF LETTERS, AT THE CRITERION RESTAURANT, ON WEDNESDAY, JULY 25, 1888. London, Society of Authors, 1888, 8vo. pp. 18.

American Ideas for English Readers, 1902.

SPEECH AT A BANQUET OF THE LIVERPOOL PHILOMATHIC SOCIETY, November 23, 1888, held at the Adelphi Hotel.

American Ideas for English Readers, 1892.

ADDRESS AT WASHINGTON CENTENARY.

The Washington Centenary Celebration in New York, April 29, 30–May 1, 1889. 8vo, New York, 1889. Address by Lowell on "Literature's Part in the Celebration."

Critic, May 4, 1889, v. 14, p. 225.

Literary and Political Addresses, 1890. Our Literature.

ADDRESS ON STUDY OF LANGUAGES.

Publications of the Modern Language Association, vol. v, no. 1. Baltimore, 1890, 8vo. Address by Lowell [on "Three Dead Languages: Hebrew, Greek, and Latin."]

Latest Literary Essays and Addresses, 1892.

BIOGRAPHIES, LETTERS, REMIN-
ISCENCES

ALPHA DELTA PHI REUNION DINNER IN NEW YORK, 1875.
New York, privately printed, 1876. Letter by Lowell.

ARBOR DAY. Edited by Robert W. Furnas. Lincoln, Ne-
braska, State Journal Co., 1888, 8vo. With a letter by
Lowell to H. L. Wood, "a tribute of friendly gratitude
for the inventor of Arbor Day."

ART OF AUTHORSHIP. Compiled and Edited by George
Bainton. New York, *Appleton*, 1890. Letter by Lowell,
p. 29.

BENTON, JOEL. Century, "Lowell's Americanism," November, 1891, v. 43, p. 120. Contains letter from Lowell
to Benton on "The World's Fair," and "Tempora
Mutantur."

BOOK-BUYER, January, 1906, v. 30, p. 231. Letter of 1887,
about Mrs. Brookfield, to the Editor of Scribner's Magazine, in which the letters of Thackeray to her first appeared, 1889.

BOOKS AND LETTERS COLLECTED BY WILLIAM HARRIS
ARNOLD OF NEW YORK. The Marion Press. Jamaica,
Queensborough, New York, 1901. Three letters by
Lowell, p. 110.

BRAINARD, CHARLES H. John Howard Payne: A Biographical Sketch of the Author of "Home, Sweet Home,"
with a narrative of the removal of his remains from
Tunis to Washington. Boston, *Cupples, Upham & Co.*,
1885. Letters by Lowell, pp. 83, 89.

BROWN, EMMA ELIZABETH. Life of James Russell Lowell. Boston, *D. Lothrop*, 1887. 12mo, pp. 354, cloth.

BULLETIN OF THE NEW YORK PUBLIC LIBRARY. Letters by Lowell to Evert Augustus Duyckinck, v. 2, p. 444, v. 4, p. 339, nine letters in all, written from 1843 to 1854.

CLARKE, MARY A. Century, February, 1896, v. 51, p. 545. Three letters by Lowell.

CRITIC, THE.

Letter on International Copyright to Miss Kate Field, reprinted from *Kate Field's Washington* of May 21, 1890, May 24, 1890, v. 13, p. 252.

Letter of advice to Mrs. H. B. Stowe, v. 14, p. 11.

Letter, September 12, 1891, v. 16, p. 134.

Letter to Robert Collyer, November 19, 1891, v. 16, p. 292.

Letters, November 28, 1891, v. 16, p. 291.

Letter to Joseph B. Gilder, November 4, 1893, v. 23, p. 289.

Letter, December 30, 1893, v. 23, p. 428.

CURTIS, GEORGE WILLIAM. James Russell Lowell: an Address [at the Brooklyn Institute, February 22, 1892]. New York, *Harpers*, 1892. 32mo, pp. 64, cloth. Reprinted in Orations and Addresses, v. 3, 1894.

MEMORIALS OF TWO FRIENDS, JAMES RUSSELL LOWELL: 1819–1891, George William Curtis: 1824–1892. New York, Privately Printed [The Gillispie Press], 1902. 50 copies printed. Contains Curtis on Lowell, Lowell's "Epistle to George William Curtis," and Charles Eliot Norton's "Life and Character of George William Curtis."

EXECUTIVE DOCUMENTS, 3d Session, 45th Congress, 1878–79. Volume 1. Foreign Relations of the United States. Washington, 1879. Lowell's letters from Spain to the State Department.

Critic, September, 1898, v. 33, p. 171. "Mr. Lowell in Spain."

Century, November, 1898, v. 57, p. 140. "Lowell's Impressionsof Spain. From Hitherto Unpublished Official Despatches. With a prefatory note on Spanish Politics by Hon. A. A. Adee."

Impressions of Spain. Compiled by Joseph B. Gilder, with an introduction by A. A. Adee. Boston, *Houghton, Mifflin & Co.*, 1899. 12mo, pp. ix, 107, portrait. Contains Lowell's letters from Spain to the State Department.

FARRAR, FREDERICK WILLIAM. Independent, "Reminiscences of Lowell," May 20, 1897, v. 49, p. 633.

GILL, WILLIAM F. Life of Edgar Allan Poe. New York, *Appleton*, 1877. Letters by Lowell.

GORDON, LADY CAMILLA. Suffolk Tales and Other Stories. London, 1897. Includes "A Few Personal Reminiscences of James Russell Lowell."

GREENSLET, FERRIS. James Russell Lowell: His Life and Work. Boston, *Houghton, Mifflin & Co.*, 1905. 12mo, pp. 309, cloth.

GRISWOLD, RUFUS W., Passages from the Correspondence of. Cambridge, 1901. Letter of Lowell, p. 151.

HALE, EDWARD EVERETT. Lowell and his Friends. The Outlook, February 5 to December, 1898, v. 58, p. 329, to v. 60, p. 853.

James Russell Lowell and his Friends. Boston, *Houghton, Mifflin & Co.*, 1898, 8vo, pp. viii, 303.

HALE, EDWARD EVERETT, JR. James Russell Lowell. Boston, *Small, Maynard & Co.*, 1899, 24mo, pp. xviii, 128. (Beacon Biographies.) Bibliography, pp. 124–128.

HALLOWELL, MRS. ANNA D. Harper's Weekly, April 23,

1892, v. 36, p. 393. "An Episode in the Life of James Russell Lowell." Includes a dozen letters, and "A Rallying Cry for New England against the Annexation of Texas."

HARRISON, GABRIEL. John Howard Payne, Dramatist, Poet, Actor: His Life and Writings. Philadelphia, 1885, 8vo. Contains three letters by Lowell relating to the removal of the remains of Payne from Tunis to Washington.

HARRISON, JAMES A. Life and Letters of Edgar Allan Poe. New York, Crowell, 1902. Numerous letters from Lowell.

HIGGINSON, THOMAS WENTWORTH. Book and Heart: Essays on Literature and Life. New York, *Harpers*, 1897. "Lowell's Closing Years in Cambridge."
Old Cambridge. New York, *Macmillan*, 1899. Last essay is on Lowell, and includes several letters.
Part of a Man's Life. Boston, *Houghton, Mifflin & Co.*, 1905. Contains letter by Lowell.

HOUSE, EDWARD HOWARD. Harper's Weekly, September 3, 1892, v. 36, p. 850. "A First Interview with Lowell."

LETTERS OF JAMES RUSSELL LOWELL. Edited by Charles Eliot Norton. In two volumes, 8vo, New York, *Harpers*, 1894. [1893.] Portraits. Vol. I, pp. viii, 418; vol. II, pp. 464.

LETTERS OF JAMES RUSSELL LOWELL. Edited by Charles Eliot Norton. In three volumes. Boston, *Houghton, Mifflin & Co.*, 1904. Vol. I, pp. viii, 348; vol. II, pp. 409; vol. III, pp. 370. Vols. XIV, XV, XVI, Elmwood Edition of Lowell's Works. Portraits and illustrations.
"The present edition of the collected writings of James Russell Lowell has been enriched by the addition of three volumes containing his 'Letters,' edited by Charles Eliot Norton. In these three volumes are in-

cluded many letters hitherto unpublished, which have
been inserted by Professor Norton in their proper
chronological order."

LOWELL, ABBOTT LAWRENCE. Proceedings of the Massachusetts Historical Society. Second series, v. 11, p. 75.
"Memoir of James Russell Lowell." Reprinted from
the Proceedings of May and June, 1896. Cambridge,
John Wilson & Son, University Press, 1896. 8vo, paper.

MILITARY ORDER OF THE ROYAL LEGION OF THE UNITED
STATES. Massachusetts Commandery. In Memoriam:
James Russell Lowell. Boston, 1892, 8vo, pp. 8.

OREGON, SOURCES OF THE HISTORY OF. Vol. I. Correspondence and Journals of Captain Nathaniel J. Wyeth.
Eugene, University Press, 1899. Preface contains letter
by Lowell.

PARKER, CLARA M. Christian Union, "Visit to Lowell,"
v. 45, p. 1146.

POE, EDGAR ALLAN, Works of the late. With Notices of
his Life and Genius, by N. P. Willis, J. R. Lowell,
and R. W. Griswold. New York, *J. S. Redfield*, 1850.
In two volumes, 12mo.

PROCEEDINGS AT THE PRESENTATION OF A PORTRAIT OF
JOHN GREENLEAF WHITTIER to Friends' School, Provi-
dence, R. I. Cambridge, 1885. Letter and sonnet by
Lowell.

REPORT OF THE COMMITTEE OF THE ASSOCIATION OF THE
ALUMNI OF HARVARD COLLEGE, July 16, 1857. With
a statement of deficiencies in the Library of Harvard
University. Cambridge, 1858. 8vo. Report prepared
by Lowell.

ROME, THE OLD AND THE NEW, and Other Studies.
London: *Grant Richards*, 1897. Contains "A Few of
Lowell's Letters."

SAVAGE, MINOT JUDSON. Arena, "A Morning with Lowell," December, 1895, v. 15, p. 1.

SCUDDER, HORACE ELISHA. James Russell Lowell: A Biography. In two volumes. Boston, *Houghton, Mifflin & Co.*, 1901. 12mo, cloth. Vol. I, pp. ix, 455; vol. II, pp. 482. "A List of the Writings of James Russell Lowell, arranged as nearly as may be in order of Publication," pp. 421–447, vol. II.

SOLDIERS' FIELD, THE. June 10, 1890. Cambridge, 8vo, 1890. Contains inscriptions prepared by Lowell.

SPARKS FROM THE PHILOSOPHER'S STONE. By J. L. Basford. London, 1882, square 16mo. Contains letter by Lowell.

STILLMAN, WILLIAM JAMES. The Autobiography of a Journalist. In two volumes. Boston, *Houghton, Mifflin & Co.*, 1901. Chapter xiv is devoted to reminiscences of Lowell, and there are other references.

STODDARD, RICHARD HENRY. Recollections: Personal and Literary. New York, *Barnes*, 1903. Contains "At Lowell's Fireside."

STORY OF THE MEMORIAL FOUNTAIN TO SHAKESPEARE AT STRATFORD-UPON-AVON, THE. Edited by E. Clarke Davis. Cambridge, Riverside Press, 1890. Contains letter by Lowell.

SWORD AND THE PEN, THE. Daily newspaper published in the interest of the Soldiers' Home Bazaar, Boston, December 7–17, 1881. Letter from Lowell in no. 7, Dec. 14.

THE TWO HUNDRED AND FIFTIETH ANNIVERSARY OF THE SETTLEMENT OF NEWBURY, NEWBURYPORT, 1885. Letter by Lowell.

UNCLAIMED ESTATES IN ENGLAND. Contains letter by

Lowell, dated November 15, 1884, to the Secretary of State, with accompanying letters, Washington, pp. 16, 8vo. [1894 ?]

UNDERWOOD, FRANCIS HENRY. James Russell Lowell: A Biographical Sketch. Boston, *James R. Osgood & Co.*, 1882. 8vo, pp. 167. Illustrations.

Harper's Magazine, January, 1881, v. 62, p. 252. "James Russell Lowell," with illustrations.

Contemporary Review, October, 1891, v. 60, p. 477. "James Russell Lowell."

The Poet and the Man: Recollections and Appreciations of James Russell Lowell. Boston, *Lee and Shepard*, 1893. 12mo, pp. 138. Bibliography, pp. 129–133.

WHAT AMERICAN AUTHORS THINK ABOUT INTERNATIONAL COPYRIGHT. New York, 1888, 8vo. Letter by Lowell.

WOODBERRY, GEORGE EDWARD. Century, August, 1894, v. 16, p. 170. "Lowell's Letters to Poe," nine in all. Reprinted in Harrison's Ed. of Poe's Works, v. 17.

NOTICES AND CRITICISMS

ACADEMY.

"The Official Lowell." January 11, 1902, v. 62, p. 667.
"Beginnings of an Author." January 17, 1903, v. 64, p. 65.
"Littérateur, Ambassador, Patriot, Cosmopolite." July 29, 1899, v. 57, p. 113.
"A Neglected Lowell." August 5, 1899, v. 57, p. 135.

ADDRESSES. LOWELL COMMEMORATION IN ARCHITEKTEN-HAUS, Berlin, February 19, 1897, by Alois Brandl, Hermann Grimm, and James Taft Hatfield. Berlin, *Mayer & Muller*, 1897, pp. 28, 8vo.

AKERS, CHARLES.

New England Magazine, "Personal Glimpses of our New England Poets," December, 1897, v. 17, n. s., p. 446.

ANDERSON, M. B.

The Dial, v. 7, p. 241.
The Dial, v. 9, p. 95.

ATHENÆUM.

"Letters of James Russell Lowell." October 28, 1893, v. 2, p. 581.
"Last Poems." January 4, 1896, v. 1, p. 12.
"Scudder's Life." February 22, 1902, v. 12, p. 235.

ATLANTIC MONTHLY.

"Mr. Lowell's Politics." August, 1888, v. 62, p. 274.
"Mr. Lowell and the Atlantic." October, 1891, v. 68, p. 576.
"Lowell's Last Poems." February, 1896, v. 77, p. 267.
"Conversations with Mr. Lowell." January, 1897, v. 79, p. 127.

"Lowell's Temperament." December, 1902, v. 90, p. 862.

"Mr. Scudder's Life of Lowell." February, 1902, v. 89, p. 254.

BANCROFT, GEORGE.
Literary World, "Our ablest Critic," June 27, 1885, v. 16, p. 217.

BARTLETT, DAVID W.
Modern Agitators or Pen Portraits, "James Russell Lowell." New York, *Saxton*, 1855.

BARTOL, CYRUS AUGUSTUS.
Literary World, "The Songster of Elmwood," June 27, 1885, v. 16, p. 217.

BEALS, SUSAN B.
Outline Studies in James Russell Lowell, his Poetry and Prose, Chicago, *Kerr & Co.*, 1887. 16mo, pp. 32.

BENTON, JOEL.
Century, "Lowell's Americanism," November, 1891, v. 21, n. s., p. 119.

BLATHWAYT, RAYMOND.
Review of Reviews, "A Last Interview at Elmwood," October, 1891, v. 4, p. 307.

BOLTON, SARAH KNOWLES.
Famous American Authors. New York, *Crowell*, 1887, p. 156.

BOOK-BUYER.
September, 1900, v. 21, p. 78.

BOWEN, FRANCIS.
North American Review, "The New Timon," April, 1847, v. 64, p. 460.

The same "Humorous and Satirical Poetry," January, 1849, v. 68, p. 183.

BRIGGS, C. F.
Journeys to Homes of American Authors. New York, *Putnams*, 1853.

BROOKS, CHARLES TIMOTHY.
Christian Examiner, "Conversations on the Old Poets," March, 1845, v. 38, p. 211.

BROWN, EMMA ELIZABETH.
Life of James Russell Lowell. Boston, *Lothrop*, 1887, 12mo, pp. 354.

BROWNSON, ORESTES AUGUSTUS.
Works, v. 19, p. 308.

BUNGAY, GEORGE W.
Off-hand Takings or Crayon Sketches of Noticeable Men of Our Age. New York, *De Witt & Davenport*, 1854.
Traits of Representative Men. New York, *Fowler & Wells*, 1882. Lowell, pp. 11–25.

BURTON, RICHARD.
Literary Leaders of America. New York, *Scribners*, 1905. Lowell, pp. 241–254.

CAMBRIDGE TRIBUNE.
Lowell Memorial Number. February 20, 1892.
Charles Eliot Norton, "Mr. Lowell and Cambridge."
Charlotte Fiske Bates, "Lowell's Elmwood."
Frank L. Chapman, "Lowell in Politics."
Thomas Wentworth Higginson, "Tribute to James Russell Lowell."
Andrew P. Peabody, "Mr. Lowell as a Teacher."
Oliver Wendell Holmes, "A Long and Interesting Friendship."
Sarah Warner Brooks, "Lowell as a Helpful and Kindly Critic."
William Winter, "Lowell and Longfellow."
Charles W. Eliot, "Lowell as a Professor."

Christopher P. Cranch, "One of Lowell's Intimate Friends."

Alexander McKenzie, "A Few Recollections."

CAPEN, OLIVER BRONSON.
Country Homes of Famous Americans. New York, *Doubleday, Page & Co.*, 1905.

CARY, ELIZABETH LUTHER.
Book-Buyer, July, 1899, v. 18, p. 431.

CHADWICK, JOHN WHITE.
Forum, "Lowell in his Letters," March, 1894, v. 17, p. 114.
Nation, "Scudder's Lowell," November 28, 1901, v. 73, p. 416.
Unitarian Review, "Lowell's Mind and Art: a Criticism," v. 63, p. 456.

CHAMBERLAIN, D. H.
New Englander, December, 1891, v. 55, p. 477.

CHENEY, JOHN VANCE.
That Dome in Air: Thoughts on Poetry and the Poets. Chicago, *McClurg*, 1895. Lowell, pp. 61–99.
Chautauquan, "Writings of Lowell," v. 16, p. 554.
Cornhill Magazine, "Lowell's Poems," January, 1875, v. 31, p. 65. Same, Littell's Living Age, February 6, 1875, v. 124, p. 387.

CORTISSOZ, ROYAL.
Century, "Some Writers of Good Letters," March, 1897, v. 31, p. 780.

CRANCH, CHRISTOPHER PEARSE.
Critic, February 23, 1889, v. 14, p. 93.

CRITIC.
"The Authorship of 'Richard III,'" March 5, 1887, v. 7, p. 109.

"Speech at Liverpool," December 15, 1888, v. 13, p. 305.

"Mr. Lowell on Mr. Cleveland," December 28, 1889, v. 15, p. 327.

"Seventieth Birthday," Special Lowell number, February 23; also March 2, 1889, v. 14, pp. 85, 104.

"The Riverside Lowell," February, 1891, v. 15, p. 91.

"Old English Dramatists," January 7, 1893, v. 19, p. 1.

"Underwood's Lowell," April 29, 1893, v. 19, p. 274.

"Celebration of Lowell's Seventy-third Birthday," March 5, 1892, v. 20, p. 147.

"Lowell as Poet and Man" [Underwood's Book], April 19, 1893, v. 22, p. 274.

Letters as edited by Norton, November 4, 1893, v. 23, p. 282.

"The Lowell Memorial," December 2, 16, 23, 1893, v. 23, p. 365, 400, 414.

"Memorial Park," November 27, 1897, v. 31, p. 331.

"Hale's Lowell and his Friends," June, 1899, v. 34, p. 521.

"Scudder's Biography," February, 1902, v. 40, p. 121.

George E. Woodberry, "James Russell Lowell at Elmwood," March 27, 1886, v. 8, p. 151.

Thomas Hughes, "Mr. Lowell's 'Fable' and 'Unhappy Lot,'" March 27, 1886, v. 8, p. 152.

"International Copyright," May 24, 1890, v. 13, p. 262.

"Prof. Norton's Tribute to Lowell," May 6, 1893, v. 22, p. 287.

CURRENT LITERATURE.

"Talkative Aspect of Lowell's Genius," December, 1905, v. 39, p. 614.

CURTIS, GEORGE WILLIAM.

Harper's Magazine, "Mr. Lowell's Birmingham Address," March, 1881, v. 70, p. 644.

James Russell Lowell: An Address. Brooklyn Institute, February 22, 1892. New York, *Harpers*, 1892.

The Same. Orations and Addresses, v. 3, 1894.

DENNETT, J. R.

Nation, "Lowell's Essays," April 21, 1870, v. 10, p. 258.

DURGEE, GEORGE W. W.

Book-Buyer,"First Editions of Lowell," July, 1899, v. 18, p. 436.

EDINBURGH REVIEW.

"James Russell Lowell," January, 1900, v. 191, p. 157.

"The Writings of James Russell Lowell," October, 1891, v. 174, p. 377. Same, Littell's Living Age, December 5, 1891, v. 191, p. 579.

ELIOT, CHARLES WILLIAM.

Annual Report of the President and Treasurer of Harvard College, 1890–91, p. 3.

EMERSON, OLIVER FARRAR.

Dial, "James Russell Lowell, 1819–1891," September, 1891, v. 12, p. 183.

FARRAR, FREDERIC WILLIAM.

Forum, "English Estimate of Lowell," October, 1891, v. 12, p. 141.

Independent, "Reminiscences of Lowell," May 20, 1897, v. 49, p. 633.

FELTON, CORNELIUS CONWAY.

North American Review, "Lowell's Poems," April, 1844, v. 58, p. 283.

FRENCH, C. N.

Illustrated American, "Elmwood," August 1, 1896, v. 20, p. 179.

GAMBLE, W. M.

Conservative Review, v. 2, p. 149.

GILMORE, JOSEPH HENRY.
Chautauquan, "Biglow Papers," April, 1896, v. 23, p. 19.

GINER DE LOS RIOS, FRANCISCO.
Boletin de la institucion libre de enseñanza, August 31, 1891, p. 241.

GODKIN, EDWIN LAWRENCE.
Nation, "Mr. Lowell and the Irish," May 25, 1882, v. 34, p. 438.
Nation, "The Reasons why Mr. Lowell should be recalled," June 1, 1882, v. 34, p. 457.
Nation, "Mr. Lowell," May 28, 1885, v. 40, p. 436.

GORDON, LADY CAMILLA.
Suffolk Tales and Other Stories, "A Few Personal Reminiscences of James Russell Lowell," London, 1897, p. 135.

GRAHAM'S MAGAZINE.
"Lowell's Poems," April, 1842, v. 20, p. 195.

GREEN, GEORGE WALTON.
International Review, "Mr. Lowell and the Irish-American Suspects," June, 1882, v. 12, p. 592.

GRISWOLD, RUFUS WILMOT.
Poets and Poetry of America, Philadelphia, *Parry & McMillan*, 1858.

GRISWOLD, HATTIE TYNG.
Home Life of American Authors, Chicago, *McClurg*, 1887.
Personal Sketches of Recent Authors, Chicago, *McClurg*, 1899.

GRUBB, EDWARD.
New England Magazine, "The Socialism of James Russell Lowell," July, 1892, v. 6, n. s., p. 676.

HALE, EDWARD EVERETT.

New England Magazine, October, 1891, v. 5, n. s., p. 183.

Outlook, "Lowell and his Friends," February to December, 1898, vv. 59, 60.

HALE, EDWARD EVERETT, JR.

Reader, "Literary Work of Lowell," July, 1905, v. 6, p. 233.

HALLOWELL, ANNA D.

Harper's Weekly, "An Episode in the Life of James Russell Lowell," April 23, 1892, v. 36, p. 393.

HARPER'S MAGAZINE.

"Works of Lowell," June, 1891, v. 83, p. 152.

Birmingham address. Easy Chair, March, 1885, v. 70, p. 644.

"One View of Lowell," November, 1891, v. 83, p. 961.

Lowell's death, Easy Chair, November, 1891, v. 83, p. 961.

HARPER'S WEEKLY.

"Lowell and Howells," January 25, 1902, v. 46, p. 101.

HARRIS, JOEL CHANDLER.

Critic, March 2, 1889, v. 14, p. 105.

HARRISON, JAMES A.

Critic, February 23, 1889, v. 14, p. 90.

HART, JAMES MORGAN.

Publications Modern Language Association [Address in Memory of Lowell], Baltimore, 1892, v. 7, p. 25.

HARTE, BRET.

New Review, "A Few Words about Lowell," September, 1891, v. 5, p. 193.

HARVARD GRADUATES' MAGAZINE.

March, 1902, v. 10, p. 345.

HAWEIS, HUGH REGINALD.
   Gentleman's Magazine, "James Russell Lowell, Poet and Essayist," October, November, 1880, v. 249 (n. s. 25), pp. 464, 544. Same, Littell's Living Age, October 30, November 20, 1880, v. 147, pp. 363, 564.
   American Humorists, London, *Chatto & Windus*, 1882, p. 75.

HIGGINSON, THOMAS WENTWORTH.
   Critic, "Lowell in Cambridge," February 23, 1889, v. 14, p. 90.
   Nation, August 13, 1891, v. 53, p. 116.
   Nation, "Lowell's Letters," December 28, 1893, v. 57, p. 488.
   Independent, "Lowell and Mr. Smalley," May 14, 1896, v. 48, p. 645.
   Book and Heart, "Lowell's Closing Years in Cambridge," 1897.
   Old Cambridge, New York, *Macmillan*, 1899.
   Outlook, "Greenslet's Life of Lowell," November 11, 1905, v. 81, p. 625.

HILLARD, GEORGE STILLMAN.
   North American Review, "A Year's Life," April, 1841, v. 52, p. 452.

HOLLAND, FREDERIC MAY.
   New England Magazine, "Reading Dante with Lowell," January, 1896, v. 13, n. s., p. 575.

HOMES OF AMERICAN AUTHORS.
   New York, *Putnams*, 1852.

HOUSE, EDWARD HOWARD.
   Harper's Weekly, "A First Interview with Lowell," September 3, 1892, v. 36, p. 850.

HOWE, MARK ANTONY DE WOLFE.
   Atlantic Monthly, "Last Poems," February, 1896, v. 77, p. 267.

Bookman, "Whittier and Lowell," March, 1898, v. 7, p. 35.

American Bookmen, New York, *Dodd, Mead & Co.*, 1898.

Literature, "Lowell and his Friends," June 16, 1899, v. 4, p. 537.

HOWELLS, WILLIAM DEAN.

Atlantic Monthly, "Poetical Works," January, 1877, v. 39, p. 93.

Scribner's Magazine, "A Personal Retrospect of James Russell Lowell," September, 1900, v. 28, p. 363.

Current Literature, January, 1901, v. 30, p. 48.

Literary Friends and Acquaintances, "Studies of Lowell," 1900.

HORWILL, HERBERT W.

New England Magazine, "Lowell's Influence in England," November, 1902, v. 27, n. s., p. 321.

HUBBARD, ELBERT.

Little Journeys to Homes of American Authors, v. 2, p. 123.

HUGHES, THOMAS.

Critic, "Fable for Critics," v. 8, p. 152.

HUNTINGTON, TULEY FRANCIS.

Dial, "Lowell and his Friends," June 1, 1899, v. 26, p. 367.

International Review, "James Russell Lowell and Modern Literary Criticism," March, 1877, v. 4, p. 264.

JAHRBÜCHER PREUSSISCHE.

"Lowell, der Satiriker, Nachklänge amerikanische Gedachtnisreden in Berlin," v. 89, p. 133.

JAMES, HENRY.

Atlantic Monthly, January 1892, v. 69, p. 35.

Essays in London, New York, *Harpers*, 1893.

Warner's Library World's Best Literature, v. 16, 1897.

JAMESON, JOHN FRANKLIN.
    Review of Reviews, "Lowell and Public Affairs,"
    October, 1891, v. 4, p. 287.

JOHNSON, W. H.
    Critic, February, 1902, v. 40, p. 121.

JONES, R. D.
    Review of Reviews, "Lowell and the Public Schools,"
    October, 1891, v. 4, p. 294.

KENYON, J. B.
    Methodist Review, "Correspondence of Lowell,"
    v. 61, p. 269.

KEYSER, LEANDER SYLVESTER.
    New England Magazine, "Lowell and the Birds,"
    November, 1891, v. 5, n. s., p. 398.

KNORTZ, KARL.
    Geschichte Nord-amerikanischen Literatur, v. 2,
    Berlin, *Hans Lüslenöder*, 1891.

KOOPMAN, HARRY LYMAN.
    Literary World, "First Editions of the 'Fable for
    Critics,'" January 8, March 5, 1898, v. 29, pp. 9, 74.

LARREMORE, W.
    Overland Monthly, "Lowell the Poet," v. 10, n. s.,
    p. 271.

LAWTON, WILLIAM CRANSTON.
    Lippincott's Magazine, "Our Fullest Throat of Song,"
    November, 1895, v. 56, p. 717.
    The New England Poets: A Study of Emerson, Haw-
    thorne, Longfellow, Whittier, Lowell, Holmes, New
    York, 1898.

LEWIN, WALTER.
    Academy, August 22, 1891, v. 40, p. 155.
    Academy, "Letters of Lowell," December 9, 1893,
    v. 44, p. 505.

LITERARY WORLD. Lowell Number, June 27, 1885, v. 16, p. 217.
> Memorial to Lowell, March 19, 1898, v. 29, p. 89.

LITTELL'S LIVING AGE.
> "The Death of Mr. Lowell," September 19, 1891, v. 190, p. 760. From The London Times.

LIVINGSTON, LUTHER S.
> Bookman, "First Books of Some American Authors," October, 1898, v. 8, p. 138.

LOCKWOOD, FERRIS.
> Scribner's Monthly, "Mr. Lowell on Art Principles," February, 1894, v. 15, p. 186.

LOW, SYDNEY.
> Fortnightly Review, "Lowell in his Poetry," September, 1891, v. 56, p. 310.

LOWE , ABBOTT LAWRENCE.
> Proceedings Massachusetts Historical Society, second series, v. 11, p. 75.

MABIE, HAMILTON WRIGHT.
> My Study Fire, second series, "Lowell's Letters," New York, *Dodd, Mead & Co.*, 1894.

MACLEOD, A.
> Catholic Presbyterian, v. 8, p. 125.

McCARTHY, JUSTIN.
> St. James Magazine, v. 34, p. 427.

MEAD, EDWIN DOAK.
> New England Magazine, "Lowell's Pioneer," October, 1891, v. 5, n. s., p. 235.

MEANS, D. MacG.
> Nation, "Lowell the Patriot," August 20, 1891, v. 53, p. 136.

MERRILL, GEORGE B.
　　James Russell Lowell: A Paper read at the annual
dinner Harvard Club of San Francisco, October 22, 1891.
San Francisco, Harvard Club, 1891.

MEYNELL, ALICE.
　　The Rhythm of Life, and Other Essays, London, *Lane*,
1893.

MIMS, E.
　　South Atlantic Quarterly, "Lowell as a Citizen," January, 1902, v. 1, p. 27.

MORSE, JAMES HERBERT.
　　Critic, February 23, 1889, v. 14, p. 88.

MOULTON, LOUISE CHANDLER.
　　The Author, v. 3, p. 36.

NADAL, EHRMAN SYME.
　　Critic, "Some Impressions of Mr. Lowell," February
25, 1893, v. 19, p. 105.

NATION.
　　"James Russell Lowell," August 13, 1891, v. 53, p. 116.
　　"Hale's Lowell," June 1, 1899, v. 68, p. 420.
　　"Scudder's Lowell," November 28, 1901, v. 73, p. 416.
　　"Lowell the Reformer," January 1, 1903, v. 76, p. 14.
　　"Greenslet's Lowell," March 1, 8, 1906.

NATIONAL MAGAZINE.
　　"Lowell and Eugene Field," March, 1902, v. 15,
p. 674.

NEW ENGLANDER.
　　"Lowell and Browning," January, 1870, v. 29, p. 125.

NORTON, CHARLES ELIOT.
　　Harper's Magazine, "James Russell Lowell," May,
1893, v. 86, p. 846.
　　Harper's Magazine, "Letters of Lowell," September,
1893, v. 87, p. 553.

OSSOLI, MARGARET FULLER.
Art, Literature, and the Drama, "American Literature," Boston, 1859, p. 308.

OUTLOOK.
"Lowell as Man and Embassador," April 3, 1897, v. 55, p. 881.

PALMER, ROUNDELL.
International Review, "Lowell and Modern Criticism," 1877, v. 4, p. 264.

PARKER, CLARA M.
Christian Union, "Visit to Lowell," v. 45, p. 1146.

PARTON, JAMES.
Literary World, "Mr. Lowell's Return," June 27, 1885, v. 16, p. 219.

PAYNE, WILLIAM MORTON.
Dial, "Scudder's Life," November 1, 1901, v. 31, p. 312.

POE, EDGAR ALLAN.
"Poems of Lowell," Harrison Ed., v. 4. Also v. 11, p. 243.
"Autobiography," Harrison Ed., v. 15.
"Poe and his Friends: Letters relating to Poe," v. 17, p. 158.

POET-LORE.
"Lowell's 'Vision of Sir Launfal,'" January, 1894, v. 6, p. 47.

POND, GEORGE EDWARD.
Liber Scriptorum, "Lowell at Harvard," New York, Author's Club, 1893, p. 456.

POWERS, HORATIO NELSON.
Homes of the Elder Poets, p. 162.

QUARTERLY REVIEW.
"James Russell Lowell," July, 1902, v. 196, p. 61.
The Same, Littell's Living Age, September 13, 1902,
v. 234, p. 641.

RIANO, E. GAYANGAS DE.
Century, "Lowell and his Spanish Friends; with an
Unpublished Poem," June, 1900, v. 38, p. 292.

RICE, WALLACE.
Dial, "Lowell on Human Liberty," January 1, 1903,
v. 34, p. 14.

RIDEING, WILLIAM HENRY.
Cosmopolitan, "Boyhood of Lowell," v. 4, p. 253.

ROOSEVELT, THEODORE.
Critic, February 23, 1889, v. 14, p. 86.

SANBORN, FRANKLIN BENJAMIN.
New England Magazine, "Home and Haunts of
Lowell," November, 1891, v. 5, n. s., p. 275.

SATURDAY REVIEW.
"An American Cassandra," August 4, 1888, v. 66,
p. 147.

SAVAGE, MINOT JUDSON.
Arena, "The Religion of Lowell's Poems," May, 1894,
v. 9, p. 705.
The Same, "A Morning with Lowell," December,
1895, v. 15, p. 1.

SCUDDER, HORACE ELISHA.
Atlantic Monthly, "Lowell, Brooks and Gray in their
Letters," January, 1894, v. 73, p. 124.
Proceedings American Academy of Arts and Sciences,
v. 29, p. 423.
Scribner's Magazine, "Mr. Lowell as a Teacher,"
November, 1891, v. 10, p. 645.

SHEPARD, WILLIAM.

Pen Pictures of Modern Authors, New York, *Putnams*, 1882, v. 2.

SKILDING, EUGENIA.

Atlantic Monthly, " A Poet's Yorkshire Haunts," August, 1895, v. 76, p. 181.

SMALLEY, GEORGE WASHBURN.

London Letters, "Mr. Lowell; why the English liked him and what his influence has been," New York, *Harpers*, 1890, v. 1, p. 217.

Harper's Magazine, "Mr. Lowell in England," April, 1896, v. 92, p. 788.

SMITH, GEORGE BARNETT.

Nineteenth Century, June, 1885, v. 17, p. 988. Same, Littell's Living Age, July 4, 1885, v. 166, p. 3.

SPALDING, JOHN LANCASTER.

Catholic World, "A Poet among the Poets," April, 1876, v. 23, p. 14.

SOUTHERN REVIEW.

"Life and Works," 1875, v. 18, p. 385.

SPECTATOR.

"Mr. Lowell's Conundrum," February 2, 1884, p. 148.

"Mr. Lowell on the Coming King," October 11, 1884, p. 1338. The Same, Littell's Living Age, November 8, 1884, v. 163, p. 379.

STEAD, WILLIAM THOMAS.

James Russell Lowell; his message, and how it helped me. London, 1891, 16mo, pp. 64.

STEARNS, FRANK PRESTON.

Cambridge Sketches, Philadelphia, *Lippincott*, 1905.

Modern English Prose Authors. New York, *Putnams*, 1897. Appendix : " Lowell on Carlyle's ' Frederick.' "

STEDMAN, EDMUND CLARENCE.
Century, May, 1882, v. 2, p. 97. Same in "Poets of America."

STEUART, J. H.
Letters to Living Authors, 1890.

STEWART, GEORGE.
Evenings in a Library.
Arena, October, 1891, v. 4, p. 513.
Essays from Reviews, Quebec, *Dawson*, 1892.

STILLMAN, WILLIAM JAMES.
Nation, September 17, 1891, v. 53, p. 211.
Atlantic Monthly, "A Few of Lowell's Letters," December, 1892, v. 70, p. 744.
Old Rome and the New, "A Few of Lowell's Letters," London, *Grant Richards*, 1897.
Autobiography of a Journalist, chap. 14. Boston, *Houghton, Miffllin & Co.*, 1901.

STODDARD, RICHARD HENRY.
North American Review, October, 1891, v. 153, p. 460.
Poets' Homes, first series, Boston, *Lothrop*, 1877.

STORY, WILLIAM WETMORE.
Critic, March 2, 1889, v. 14, p. 105.
Lippincott's Magazine, October, 1892, v. 50, p. 534.
Recollections, Personal and Literary, "At Lowell's Fireside;" New York, *Barnes*, 1903.
The Author, v. 3, p. 110.

SULPIUS, FRIEDRICH VON.
"Etwas von Yankeesatiriker, James Russell Lowell," Beilage zur Allgemeinen Zeitung, 1897, v. 94. München, 1897, p. 5.

SWIFT, LINDSAY.
Book-Buyer, "Lowell's Diplomatic Career," September, 1900, v. 2, p. 92.

TEMPLE BAR.
"James Russell Lowell," September, 1892, v. 96, p. 88.
The Same, Littell's Living Age, November 12, 1892,
v. 195, p. 416.

TAYLOR, BAYARD.
Critical Essays, New York, *Putnams*, 1880.

THOMPSON, MAURICE.
Critic, February 23, 1889, v. 14, p. 86.

TRAILL, HENRY DUFF.
Fortnightly Review, "Mr. J. R. Lowell," July, 1885,
v. 44, p. 79; The Same, Littell's Living Age, August 1,
1885, v. 166, p. 280.

TRAUBEL, HORACE.
Poet-Lore, "Lowell, Whitman; a Contrast," January
15, 1892, v. 4, p. 22.

UNDERWOOD, FRANCIS HENRY.
Good Words, v. 28, p. 521.
Harper's Magazine, January, 1881, v. 62, p. 252.
Contemporary, October, 1891, v. 60, p. 477.
James Russell Lowell; a Biographical Sketch, Boston,
Osgood, 1882.
The Poet and the Man; Recollections and Apprecia-
tions of James Russell Lowell, Boston, *Lee & Shepard*,
1893.
Our Day, "Lowell as a Reformer and Poet," Novem-
ber, December, 1891, v. 8, pp. 347, 444.

WARNER, CHARLES DUDLEY.
Literary World, "The Real American at his best,"
June 27, 1885, v. 16, p. 219.
Critic, February 23, 1889, v. 14, p. 85.

WATSON, WILLIAM.
Excursions in Criticism, "Lowell as a Critic," London,
Lane, 1893.

WATTS-DUNTON, THEODORE.
    Athenæum, v. 2, p. 257.

WENDELL, BARRETT.
    Stelligeri, "Lowell as a Teacher," New York, *Scribners*, 1893.

WHIPPLE, EDWIN PERCY.
    Harper's Magazine, March, 1876, v. 52, p. 516.
    Outlooks on Society, "Lowell as a Prose Writer," Boston, *Ticknor*, 1888.

WILKINSON, WILLIAM CLEAVER.
    Baptist Quarterly, "The Cathedral," v. 14, p. 374.
    The Same, "Hours at Home," v. 10, p. 541.
    Scribner's Magazine, May, June, July, 1872, v. 4, o. s., pp. 75, 227, 339.
    A Free Lance in the Field of Life and Letters, "Mr. Lowell's Poetry," "Mr. Lowell's 'Cathedral,'" "Mr. Lowell's Prose," New York, *Funk & Wagnalls*, 1874.

WILL, THOMAS ELMER.
    Arena, "Poet of Freedom," March, 1904, v. 31, p. 262.

WINCHESTER, CALEB THOMAS.
    Review of Reviews, "Lowell as a Man of Letters," October, 1891, v. 4, p. 291.

WISTER, S. B.
    Atlantic Monthly, "Conversations with Mr. Lowell," January, 1897, v. 79, p. 127.

WOODBERRY, GEORGE EDWARD.
    Critic, "Lowell at Elmwood," v. 8. p. 151.
    Nation, "Mr. Lowell's new Volume," December 23, 1886, v. 43, p. 525.
    Atlantic Monthly, "Mr. Lowell on Izaak Walton," February, 1890, v. 65, p. 266.
    Century, November, 1891, v. 21, n. s., p. 113.

Scribner's Magazine, "Lowell's Letters to Poe," August, 1894, v. 16, p. 170.

Makers of Literature, New York, *Macmillan*, 1900.

Authors at Home, New York, *Scribners*, 1889.

WRIGHT, HENRIETTA CHRISTIAN.
Children's Stories in American Literature, New York, *Scribners*, 1895, Lowell, pp. 203–205.

WRITER, "Personal Tributes to Lowell," September, October, 1891, v. 5, pp. 185, 210.

MANUSCRIPTS

A large quantity of Lowell's notebooks, manuscripts of lectures, newspaper clippings of lectures, letters, and other materials, have been given by Professor Charles Eliot Norton to the library of Harvard University. This collection is especially rich in letters from Lowell's numerous friends and correspondents. In his letter of presentation Professor Norton describes these letters:

"There are thirteen (13) portfolios containing letters addressed to him by American correspondents for the most part previously to his being sent to Spain as our minister. The letters in these portfolios are arranged in alphabetical order, and many of them are of value as autographs, and of interest as illustrating the conditions of American literature from about the middle of the last century onward. Many of them contain interesting matter concerning the literary projects of a time that was full of them, both in New York and in Boston. The little group of authors who tried to make New York a literary centre, from 1840 to 1850, and whose names even now are almost forgotten, are well represented in the letters of Duyckinck, Cornelius Matthews, James, and others. There are a number of letters relating to the early years of the *Atlantic Monthly;* and you will see that there is a very considerable parcel of letters of Dr. Holmes, and what is perhaps of still more interest, a yet larger parcel of letters of John Holmes. There is also a number of Whittier's letters and poems.

" But, beside the literary interests which are represented in these letters, the anti-slavery interests are also largely illustrated by a very considerable number of letters of Edmund Quincy, of Wendell Phillips, and of others, — the leaders in that cause.

"Both these groups of letters are imperfect, because of many having been returned to their writers, or to the representatives of their writers. Perhaps the most important letters of early years which are missing here are those of Charles F. Briggs, who at the time of Mr. Lowell's beginnings in literature was his closest friend and most frequent correspondent. His letters have gone back to his family, who desired them. In the case of some other writers, themselves dead, but who have living representatives, I have obtained permission to retain their letters, and to give them to the college. The most important case of this kind is that of Mr. Richard Grant White, whose numerous letters are of more than usual interest.

"In addition to these portfolios are two containing the letters of numerous English correspondents, of which perhaps the most interesting are the numerous letters of Judge Thomas Hughes; but there are many others of literary or other interest. These also are arranged in alphabetical order, but there are two portfolios in which the letters are not arranged alphabetically, but chronologically. They are of late years, — 1885 to 1890, — and the letters are for the most part mere notes, of more interest for their writer's sake than for their contents."